THE JOHNS HOPKINS UNIVERSITY STUDIES IN
HISTORICAL AND POLITICAL SCIENCE

Under the Direction of the Departments of History,
Political Economy, and Political Science

SERIES LXXVIII   NUMBER 2
(1960)

THE UNION PACIFIC RAILROAD

A Case in Premature Enterprise

THE UNION PACIFIC RAILROAD

A Case in Premature Enterprise

By

ROBERT WILLIAM FOGEL

BALTIMORE

THE JOHNS HOPKINS PRESS

1960

© 1960, The Johns Hopkins Press, Baltimore 18, Md.
Second printing, 1961
Printed in the United States of America
Library of Congress Catalog Card No. 60–14850

This book has been brought to publication with the
assistance of a grant from The Ford Foundation.

TO

MY PARENTS

PREFACE

This study differs from previous histories of the Union Pacific in four main respects:

First, it suggests that the progress of legislation on a Pacific railroad was marked not by a headlong flight from proposals for a government enterprise but by the difficulty Congress exhibited in breaking away from such schemes.

Second, it introduces a considerable amount of new material controverting the traditional explanation of the ruin of the railroad company. The new material includes a detailed summary of the difficulties faced by the promoters in raising the private capital needed for construction; neglected abstracts of the books of the Union Pacific and the Credit Mobilier which provide a new basis for estimating the cost of the road and the profit of the promoters; and various considerations bearing on the nature and extent of the risk faced by the promoters. This material makes it possible to quantify the market's evaluation of the probability that the Union Pacific Railroad Company would fail and to project a " justifiable " profit against which the actual profit of the promoters can be judged.

Third, it tests the economic wisdom of the government's decision to intervene in the building of the railroad by estimating the social rate of return on the construction expenditure and by evaluating the efficiency of the particular method of financing projected by Congress.

Fourth, it draws on formal economic theory in the determination and analysis of historical facts. Interest theory is combined with the theory of a " fair game " to deduce, from the market price of the railroad's first-mortgage bonds, the market's evaluation of the probability that the Union Pacific would fail. The theory of rent forms the basis for the estimation of the social rate of return on the capital invested in the railroad. The concept of present value is used in the determination of the relative efficiency of the various proposals that were put forth for the financing and construction of a Pacific road.

9

By and large, economic historians have rejected the pleas that have been made for a greater use of theory in the study of history. This rejection has been justified on the basis of the static character, the timelessness, the simplifications of many economic models. However, these limitations of economic models do not create a presumption against the applicability of theory to historical problems. To rule out the use of formal theory in the study of history, it is necessary to demonstrate the existence of a superior alternative. Yet the alternative of a purely factual presentation of economic history does not exist. As Professor Machlup has stressed, many things presented as facts are really disguised (and often quite thinly disguised) theories.[1] For example, the frequently met statement that the promoters of the Union Pacific engaged in profiteering is not a factual statement but a judgement based on an assumed relationship among the size of the profit of the promoters, the size of their investment and the degree of risk that they faced. Indeed, once the historian passes beyond the random collection of facts to the selection and linking of facts, theory is inevitably involved. The only real alternative to the use of formal theory in historical presentations is a reliance on *implicit* or *casual theory*; that is, the choice is not between theory and something else but between different kinds of theory. The advantage of formal theory over casual theory is that the former is more explicit in its assumptions and more systematic in its development.

Theory can be as helpful in the determination of facts as it can be in the explanation of them. The research worker in economic history rarely has the good fortune to find the evidence bearing on a given question to be a neat collection of unequivocal, consistent items. On the contrary, he is, as a rule, faced with conflicting and mutually exclusive items all of which claim the title of " fact." Thus, in the case of the Union Pacific we find a number of contradictory statements from reliable contemporary sources concerning the extent of the risk that confronted the promoters of the railroad. In cases such as this, theory can frequently be of great service by revealing the internal consistency or inconsistency in an alleged set of facts,

[1] Fritz Machlup, *The Political Economy of Monopoly* (Baltimore: Johns Hopkins Press, 1952), pp. 448-54.

thereby providing a logical foundation for choosing between conflicting observations.

Formal theory is not a magic wand. Not all problems in economic history lend themselves to theoretical manipulation. It is impossible to foresee the particular circumstances under which various theoretical constructs will be of use. However, if the limitations of theory are recognized, if theory is used to analyze specific problems rather than to buttress grandiose generalizations, and if the assumptions of the analysis are formulated on the basis of a careful consideration of the available institutional and empirical evidence, theory may be of much greater use in the study of economic history than has been generally realized.

Many topics that might have been dealt with in a more general history of the Union Pacific have been omitted or treated in a cursory manner. No attempt was made to discuss the protracted debate on routes or to record the almost endless maneuvers on the various bills that preceded the Pacific Railroad Acts of 1862 and 1864. The bribery aspects of the Credit Mobilier affair are alluded to only in passing. The history of the physical progress of construction is limited to the minimum required to understand the problem of funds. Restricted treatment of these and other questions was necessary to sharpen the focus on the questions of public economic policy posed by premature enterprise and to avoid repeating what is already well known.

My first debt is to Professor Carter Goodrich of Columbia University who suggested the topic of this study and supervised my work on it. His detailed criticisms improved both the style and content of the pages that follow. My obligation to Professor Goodrich extends beyond the limits of this volume. His discerning, suggestive lectures and reading notes on American economic history stimulated my desire to work in this field and provided me with an invaluable foundation for further study.

I am also indebted to Professors James K. Kindahl and Edwin S. Mills of The Johns Hopkins University for many extended discussions (in the case of Dr. Kindahl, on almost a daily basis) over a period of six months. These discussions were particularly helpful in clarifying some of the theoretical considerations involved in the calculation of the " justifiable " profit of the promoters and the estimation of the social rate of return on the Union Pacific investment. Professors G. Heberton Evans, Jr. and Simon Kuznets of The Johns Hopkins University read a late draft. Their suggestions clarified several ambiguous formulations. Mr. James Weinstein read and helped edit a number of drafts of the first two chapters. The final draft was edited by Mr. Aldo J. Fortuna. I am grateful to my wife for her constant encouragement and for enduring the slings and arrows of protracted research.

CONTENTS

How the Issue Presented Itself
The Whitney Plan
1852-1860: The Persistence of Quasi-
Government Enterprise
The Dominance of Pragmatism
Toward an Eclectic Conclusion

The Factual Background
The problem of funds
The construction contracts
The Ames-Durant conflict
The Profit
The Nature and Extent of the Risk Faced by
the Promoters
The Fundamental Deficiency in the Acts of
1862 and 1864

The Social Rate of Return
The Efficiency of the Acts of 1862 and 1864

LIST OF TABLES

THE UNION PACIFIC RAILROAD

A Case in Premature Enterprise

CHAPTER I

THE PARADOX OF PREMATURE ENTERPRISE

It is not to be overlooked, that, in the judgement of many distinguished citizens, the measure is premature, and perhaps impracticable, at the present time.

Representative Hiram Walbridge

The building of the Union Pacific Railroad has earned a secure place for itself in American historiography. Every survey of American history—economic, social or political—is certain to deal with it. The traditional treatment generally focuses on one of two aspects of the building of the road. The first aspect not only centers on the significance of the road as a major milestone in the completion of the railroad network—the link that finally spanned the continent—but also stresses its importance in making possible the settlement and exploitation of the trans-Missouri West. The second centers on the Credit Mobilier scandal: the story of the enormous profits made from the " nation's pride " by the promoters of the railroad and of the huge slush fund used to curry Congressional favor. In a period of shocking corruption, the Credit Mobilier scandal was the most notorious of all, becoming a major issue in four Presidential elections, and involving a dozen Congressmen, a Secretary of the Treasury, two Vice-Presidents, a leading Presidential contender, and one man who was later to become President.[1]

However, the building of the Union Pacific can be treated from another, somewhat neglected vantage point. While this approach stresses less sensational and dramatic aspects of the road's history, it is nonetheless important especially to a generation of economists and historians reared in an era of mixed economy. That is the story of the building of the Union Pacific as a mixed enterprise. When one examines the literature

---

[1] James Ford Rhodes, *History of the United States* (New York: Macmillan Co., 1906), VII, 1-18; Nelson Trottman, *History of the Union Pacific* (New York: Ronald Press, 1923), chap. IV; J. B. Crawford, *The Credit Mobilier of America* (Boston: C. W. Calkins, 1880), chap. VIII.

on the Pacific road it is surprising how little attention is given to this feature. Though not entirely ignored, it is generally subordinated to the scandals that followed the construction of the road or to the sectional conflict that preceded it. Yet in many ways it is precisely this feature of mixed enterprise which is most germane to an understanding of the many problems involved in the financing and construction of the road and to its subsequent history. Mixed enterprise was not extraordinarily novel in the 1860's; many roads had previously been built with the participation of state and city governments, but this was one of the few occasions in which it was the federal government that was the partner.[2] Moreover, the case of the first Pacific road was unique with respect to the size of the government contribution, totalling more than $60,000,000 in government bonds and 20,000,000 acres of land—an amount which easily eclipsed any previous public aid and which was not approached until the beginning of the twentieth century.[3]

Essential to an analysis along the lines just stated is a recognition of the fact that the Union Pacific Railroad was built as a "premature" enterprise—premature, that is, when the measuring rod of its maturity and practicability was the willingness of unaided private enterprise, guided solely by the search for profits, to undertake the project. It is this quality of prematureness which, if anything can, should be considered as the core of the Union Pacific problem. The first Pacific railroad was premature not only when the first Whitney plan[4] was put before Congress in 1845 but also when the actual construction was launched after the passage of the Acts of 1862 and 1864. That the building of the road was pushed ahead although it had not yet matured as a profitable private enterprise, made governmental intervention inevitable and thus gave rise, both before and after construction, to a series of complicated issues on the relationship of government and business.

[2] The recent volume by Carter Goodrich, *Government Promotion of American Canals and Railroads, 1800-1890* (New York: Columbia University Press, 1960), is the most comprehensive study of the role of the government at the local, state and national level in the development of internal improvements during the nineteenth century.

[3] Frederick A. Cleveland and Fred Wilbur Powell, *Railroad Promotion and Capitalization in the United States* (New York: Longmans, Green, 1909), pp. 251, 257.

[4] See below, pp. 28-32.

These exceedingly difficult problems and perhaps much of the corruption, litigation and financial insolvency that was to be the fate of the Union Pacific, and other Pacific railroads, might have been avoided had the building of these roads been postponed. This possibility was suggested by Lewis H. Haney who, while granting the political reasons for the premature building of the road, doubted that it could be economically justified. In summing up the history of Pacific railroad legislation Haney stated that the roads failed, at least in large part, to achieve the purposes for which they were constructed; " that the gross gain was less than anticipated, while a net gain is doubtful." Further, wrote Haney, it was almost " certain that within two decades private enterprise " would have been ready to build them alone.[5]

But here, indeed, was the rub. For the general public and, first and foremost, the commercial and business interests (contrary to what one might expect their attitude to have been to a project dictating government intervention) were unwilling to wait even nine more months, let alone two decades. This was pointed up in 1862 when the House quickly brushed aside proposals that action on a Pacific road be delayed until the next session of Congress.[6] The general public's attitude was that the road was long overdue.

This feeling of public impatience was rooted in two general factors. The first was that the building of the road had been so long postponed. Originally put before Congress as a practical proposal in 1845, it had been bandied about for seventeen years without resolution. As public discussion became more intense and insistent, Congress seemed to become more deeply enmeshed in that local and sectional rivalry which prevented the majority sentiment in favor of the road from being embodied in law. By the mid-fifties Senator William M. Gwin of California—where the early building of a Pacific road was a make-or-break issue for politicians—could say: " The subject cannot be postponed without outraging the public sentiment of the country." [7] Two months later Gwin reiterated: [8]

---

[5] Lewis H. Haney, *A Congressional History of Railways in the United States* (2 vols., Madison, Wis.: Democrat Printing Co., 1908, 1910), II, p. 153.
[6] *Congressional Globe*, 37th Cong., 2d Sess., pp. 1707-10.
[7] *Ibid.*, 33d Cong., 1st Sess., p. 118.
[8] *Ibid.*, p. 876.

We are left in no doubt as to the judgement of the American people on this subject. The agricultural, commercial, mechanical and manufacturing interests; our statesmen who held, and now hold high places in the councils of our nation; our citizens in primary assemblies, and Legislatures of Sovereign States, have declared in its favor; and the Press, in its power, in terms not to be misunderstood, has echoed and reëchoed public opinion in its support, from one end of the Union to the other.

The second and more important factor in promoting public impatience was the attitude that regardless of whether or not the building of the road was ripe from the point of view of its profitability to the builders and owners of the road, it was not only ripe but overripe when measured by the standard of national needs. The arguments of national necessity were military and political as well as economic. Militarily, it was said, the road was necessary in order to defend our Pacific territories from foreign attack, to cope with insurrection and to aid in suppressing the Indians. In the event of war, an enemy possessing a powerful fleet could cut our sea routes to California and Oregon, and the overland trip would take at least a month—a length of time that could spell disaster. By train the trip was less than a week. The Mormon Uprising and the Mason-Slidell incident added considerable weight to this argument.[9] Politically the railroad was urged in order to cement California's ties with the Union. It was feared that without the link that a railroad would provide, California might develop as a separate entity and eventually establish itself as an independent nation. While California never seriously threatened secession, it was quick to take advantage of the fear of this possibility to press its points.[10]

Important as were the military and political considerations, it is doubtful that these alone would have sufficed to cause the nation to undertake such a gigantic and costly enterprise.

[9] *Ibid.*, 35th Cong., 1st Sess., p. 1645; *ibid.*, 35th Cong., 2d Sess., p. 52; Major General Grenville M. Dodge, *How We Built the Union Pacific Railway* (n. p., n. n., n. d.), *passim.*

[10] " I say, sir, we [California] have the power to achieve our destiny unaided and alone. Alone we feel the power to do it; but no wish is father to that thought. We would be brethren. We ask, if you would call us brethren, greet us as such—reach out your arm toward us, and let it be an arm as strong as iron, and let us unite in a fraternal and iron grasp." Rep. McDougall, *Cong. Globe Append.*, 33d Cong., 1st Sess., p. 866.

Commercial interest was the solid foundation on which the movement for a Pacific road rested. No matter how much the other points might have been reiterated—often because the military and political arguments were less grating to the Constitutional scruples of those who held that federal aid was an infringement on states rights—it was the promise of a fabulous commercial gain for the nation that spurred the incessant drive for a transcontinental road.[11] When Whitney presented his original memorial he did not fail to take account of the military and political arguments for the road, but his main stress was on the economic benefits of the project. On the one hand he argued that the building of the road would " relieve our cities from a vast amount of misery, vice, crime, and taxation" by taking " poor unfortunates to a land where they will be compelled to labor for a subsistence." Further, the road would make it possible to " settle this vast region" of the West "with an industrious and frugal people; thus, in a comparatively short space of time accomplishing what would otherwise require ages . . . and in a few years would be built up towns, cities, and villages, from the lake to the ocean. . . ." On the other hand he painted a picture of vast new commercial profits calculated to ensnare the imagination of even the most torpid merchants and manufacturers: [12]

Then the drills and sheeting of Connecticut, Rhode Island, and Massachusetts, and the other manufactures of the United States, may be transported to China in thirty days; and the teas and rich silks of China, in exchange, come back to New Orleans, to Charleston, to Washington, to Baltimore, to Philadelphia, to New York, and to Boston, in thirty days more.

Comment is unnecessary. Your honorable body will readily see the revolution to be wrought by this in the entire commerce of the world, and that this must inevitably be its greatest channel—when the rich freights from the waters of the Mississippi and the Hudson will fill to overflowing, with the products of all the earth. . . . It would be the

---

[11] With the exception of Robert R. Russel, *Improvement of Communication with the Pacific Coast as an Issue in American Politics, 1783-1864* (Cedar Rapids, Iowa: Torch Press, 1948), previous studies do not place any particular emphasis on the economic factor but merely include it along with others. Russel takes what is perhaps too extreme a position when he says: " It is extremely doubtful, however, that military and political arguments won a single vote in Congress for Pacific railway legislation." *Ibid.*, p. 295.

[12] *Ibid.*, 28th Cong., 2d Sess., p. 218.

only channel for the commerce of all the western coast of Mexico and South America, of the Sandwich Islands, Japan, all China, Manilla, Australia, Java, Singapore, Calcutta, and Bombay—not only all ours, but the commerce of all Europe, to most of these places, must pass this road. . . .

Nor was Whitney the only one to strike this note. It was in this very vein that Benton waxed grandiloquent, promising that the results of a Pacific road would be an economic glory for American cities that would pale the wonders of Tyre, Alexandria, Constantinople, Genoa, Venice, Amsterdam and London.[13] The same argument was repeated by Gwin, Rusk, Bell, Latham, McDougall, Curtis and every other proponent of the early building of the Pacific road. In fact there was hardly a session of Congress for seventeen years in which either the House or Senate was not subjected to a lecture on monumental roads of the past and the wealth they had heaped on those peoples that were bold enough to undertake the building of them.

It was these considerations that sparked the rivalry of Milwaukee, Chicago, Quincy, St. Louis, Memphis, Vicksburg, and New Orleans for the honor of becoming the Eastern terminus of the road—each city envisioning itself as thereby becoming the great commercial emporium of the West.[14] Economic considerations also underlaid the sectional conflict over the location of the routes, each section realizing the tremendous economic, and, therefore, political repercussions which the road would have on the section of the country through which the line ran. The prospect that the road would give a new impetus to the economic development of the South and improve its competitive position with the North was high inducement to that area's leadership. Some Southerners began to view it as the principal means by which to improve the South's waning strength. Concern over the growing pre-occupation with the Pacific road, as demonstrated at the Southern Commercial Convention in 1853, led the New Orleans *Delta* to comment critically that the proposal for a Pacific road had become an "Aaron's rod that swallowed up all others. This was the great panacea, which is

[13] *Ibid.*, 30th Cong., 2d Sess., p. 473.
[14] Russel, *op. cit.*, pp. 34-39.

to release the South from its bondage to the North, which is to pour untold wealth into our lap; which is to build up cities, steamships, manufactories, educate our children, and draw into our control what Mr. Bell calls ' the untold wealth of the gorgeous East '." [15]

Here then was the paradox with which the nation had to grapple: the paradox of a railroad that was both premature and late, both profitable and unprofitable, both essential and impractical. Nor was this an artificial paradox manufactured in the heat of political rhetoric. It reflected a real dichotomy between sound private investment principles and public or national economic necessity, a dichotomy that was inherent in premature enterprise. In mature enterprise the public and private interest are normally united. The first is contained in and is fulfilled as a result of the operation of the second, with private profit acting as the dynamic force which propels the work into being and insures its completion. The " invisible hand " works as it should. But in the case of the first Pacific railroad, as in all premature enterprise, the relentless compulsion of private profit was absent, and this absence created a formidable barrier to the project. The entire burden of the work rested on the public interest which alone had to provide the impelling force that would energize the enterprise. The existence of such a dichotomy gave opponents of premature construction a powerful argument. Few would contradict them when they asserted that by the principles of profitable private investment the road was sure to fail. Yet it was equally hard to deny that the road would create many new and highly lucrative business opportunities for merchants, manufacturers and farmers, thereby enriching both individuals and the nation as a whole.

The Pacific Railroad Acts of 1862 and 1864 did not resolve the paradox. They resolved the questions of whether or not the road should be built prematurely and whether or not the government should give its monies to the project, but not the seeming contradiction between the public and private interest in the line. Congress was well aware of the paradox, as even a cursory examination of the long debate will show, but its discussion never really probed the subtleties of this all too com-

[15] Quoted by Russel, *ibid.*, p. 25.

plicated problem. The tendency was rather to seize on one or another aspect of the paradox in order to use it as ammunition for or against premature construction. The Acts that climaxed the debate were measures of expediency by a Congressional majority which was anxious to get a Pacific railroad and was at last in a position to obtain it. Practical men who recognized that " the great railroad interests, and the great interests of the country had to be consulted," [16] these legislators had little time or inclination to dally with questions that bordered on the metaphysical.

To reproach Congress for not having been wiser would be inappropriate. For one thing it is much too late a date for disapprobation. For another, it asks for an understanding of issues that usually comes only with hindsight. Despite previous practical experiences, especially on state and local levels, the broader issues involved in premature and mixed enterprises were still basically unexplored in the mid-1860's. In a certain sense these issues and the problems they posed belonged more to the next century than to the one in which they appeared.

---

[16] Senator McDougall, *Cong. Globe*, 37th Cong., 2d Sess., p. 2806.

CHAPTER II

A REINTERPRETATION OF THE CONGRESSIONAL
DEBATE ON CONSTRUCTION AND OWNERSHIP

This road never could be constructed on terms applicable to ordinary roads. Every member of the committee knows that it is to be constructed through almost impassable mountains, deep ravines, canyons, gorges, and over arid and sandy plains. The Government must come forward with a liberal hand, or the enterprise must be abandoned forever.

Representative James H. Campbell

If this road is to be built at all, it must be done by the Federal Government; it must be done by the money of the Government. . . . The only question with me is, as to the most feasible way of doing so.

Senator Walter Brooke

How the Issue Presented Itself

Most studies of the Union Pacific tend to emphasize the negative fact that Congress rejected the proposal of a government road. Haney, for example, in speaking of the period up to 1850 said that " little is to be gleaned " about proposals that came before Congress for a government road " save that Congress not only did not take up such projects, but did not consider them seriously enough to devote much discussion to them. Asa Whitney's conclusion that a government railway was not desirable in connection with our political institutions was the prevailing belief." [1] Of the period after 1850 Haney said that the issue of who was to build the Pacific road " was soon settled in favor of private enterprise, assistance being furnished by the government." [2] Trottman analyses this question in a similar vein, stating that " constitutional scruples and questions of expediency stood in the way of a government-built and operated road." [3] Davis comments that " although there had been propositions before 1850 for the building and operation

[1] Haney, *op. cit.*, I, p. 263. [2] *Ibid.*, II, p. 49.
[3] Trottman, *op. cit.*, p. 6.

25

of the Pacific Railway by the United States through its governmental machinery, its own experience in building public roads
and promoting other internal improvements, and the experience
of the several states in constructing and operating canals and
railways and conducting banks had been so unfortunate, that
this work was sure to be left in private hands." [4]

In point of fact it is, of course, true that Congress did reject
the various proposals for a purely governmental road, but the
heavy and somewhat one-sided emphasis that has been placed
on this fact in analysing the relationship of the government to
the construction of the Union Pacific is open to question. It
gives a misleading impression of the way in which the problem
of the government's relationship to this premature enterprise
actually presented itself during the course of the long years of
debate. It also tends to becloud certain essential features of
the way in which the issue was finally resolved. Even the
suggestion that the issue was settled on the basis of " entrusting
the work of constructing a Pacific railroad to private capital,
aided by liberal subsidies " is incomplete. [5]

The characteristic feature of the long debate over methods of
finance and construction was not the emergence of sharply
delineated groupings with clear-cut, consistent and unyielding
positions for or against a government road. Perhaps this type
of polarization would have taken place if the debate had been
merely academic, merely concerned with the formulation of a
theoretical abstraction. Such was not the case, however. The
issue was much more mundane and specific. It was not even
as broad as the question of what role the national government
should play in the extension of the railroad network in general,
which at this time, influenced by foreign programs for railroad
development, was projecting itself onto the American scene. [6]
What was at issue was the *practical* problem of how to finance
a *specific*, unusually difficult railroad project which was viewed
as eminently desirable, if not essential, by all of the leading

[4] John P. Davis, " The Union Pacific Railway," *Annals of American Academy
of Political and Social Science*, VIII (September, 1896), p. 49 (261).
[5] Trottman, *op. cit.*, p. 8.
[6] See, for example, J. W. Scott, "A National System of Railways," *Merchants'
Magazine and Commercial Review*, XVII (December, 1847), pp. 564-71.

economic groups in all sections of the country.[7] The initial question in the debate was how such a road could be built and not whether it should be a government road. "How?" was primary. "What role for the government?" was a derived issue.

That proposals for a government role would arise once the question "How?" was posed, was only to be expected. Though plans were of the most varied sort, nearly all involved the government in one way or another. Some were more or less pure proposals for a government work. Most of the others were complex and sometimes unorthodox schemes for combining the government and private roles. Often these two elements were woven into patterns that were far too intricate to permit a categorical classification into "government work," "private work," or even "private work aided by government." They were proposals for mixed enterprise in every sense of the term.

Of course, some bills gave greater weight to the government role and others gave greater weight to the private role. But in general the governmental aspect predominated in most of the plans of the period. Until the Curtis bill of 1860 the progress of Pacific road legislation was marked not by a headlong flight from a government road but by the difficulty in getting away from that type of scheme. Many of the bills advertised as calling for a private enterprise were separated from the frankly government plans by the width of a hair, a hair that was thin enough so that they could quite convincingly be attacked as projecting essentially government works.

The issue before Congress was never really one of choosing between opposites—a government road or a private enterprise. Only one of the bills throughout the whole period asserted that it was possible to build the road as a purely private enterprise.[8] To all intents and purposes the necessity and inevitability of governmental intervention was accepted by everybody who

[7] Even Senator James Mason, arch-opponent of federal intervention, said that none could doubt that " a railroad in practical operation connecting the Atlantic with the Pacific" would be a " *desideratum*," an accomplishment " fraught with great and beneficial results to the country." *Cong. Globe*, 35th Cong., 1st Sess., p. 1601.

[8] Below, p. 41.

favored early building. The critical clashes were over *the degree* to which the government would have to intervene and *the manner* in which that intervention was to take place.

THE WHITNEY PLAN

The Whitney plan is a leading example of a scheme which, though widely advertised as a private enterprise, was saturated with governmental aspects. Private enterprise was the ground on which Congressional supporters of Whitney took their stand. All other schemes, they said, called " for the building of this work by the government directly, or to putting it indirectly on the national treasury." Only Whitney's was based on " *the principle of private enterprise and private responsibility*." [9] A government road would saddle the government with the burdensome task of going into " a full, minute and thorough examination of every point and consideration involved; whereas, in the present case, the entire responsibility and the risk of success rests upon the memorialist, and details for its successful completion must be arranged and executed by him." [10] Ostensibly the only government commitment would have been the sale of 80,000,000 acres of public land for which the government was to receive $8,000,000.[11] It was from the difference between the cost of the land to Whitney and what he might realize from the resale of the land, whose value would be enhanced as a result of the railroad, that Whitney hoped to finance the building of the enterprise.

Those who opposed the Whitney plan did not challenge the claim that it was a private enterprise. Their charge was that it was too private. They viewed it as essentially an immense swindle by which a private individual was to receive an empire in land. It was, said Representative J. B. Bowlin of Missouri, an attempt to put the states into a " humiliating condition, subject to the power of one man "; an effort to foist a " wholesale stock-jobbing concern upon the public domain "; a proposal for committing " the blood and the treasure of the nation . . . for the sole and exclusive benefit of Mr. Whitney and his assigns." [12]

[9] *Sen. Repts.* No. 194, 31st Cong., 1st Sess., (565), p. 2.
[10] *H. Repts.* No. 733, 30th Cong., 1st Sess., (526), p. 1.
[11] *Sen. Repts.* No. 194, *op. cit.*, p. 5.
[12] *Cong. Globe, Append.*, 31st Cong., 1st Sess., pp. 329-33.

There was a possibility that Whitney would reap great speculative gain since the plan contained a proviso that any land or money (from the sale of land) remaining after the completion of the road and after making up the losses that it was generally expected the road would incur during its first ten years of operation, would go to Whitney. This possibility was conceded by his Congressional supporters.[13] But the greater possibility was that Whitney would not even be able to raise the minimum amount of funds needed to complete the project. For, at the time, over sixty per cent of the land was thought to be "too poor to sustain settlement." Even the fertile land had, at the time, no economic value. It was Whitney's hope to be able to create a price through colonization.[14]

In actuality the Whitney plan was neither a "private" enterprise nor a "private" swindle. It was a proposal for a mixed enterprise. Whether Whitney could have reaped a huge personal fortune in the course of prosecuting this mixed enterprise is a moot question and not necessarily pertinent to the problem at hand. It is, however, interesting to note that Whitney never viewed the project primarily as a personal profit-making venture. As a matter of fact his original proposal was for a government owned and operated road. His reason for later suggesting that he own and operate the road was the belief that the scheme would be rejected because of objections that were being raised to a government road.[15] Whitney was

[13] The basis on which they rationalized this possibility is interesting, especially since essentially the same argument was used in connection with subsequent proposals for government aid.

"Admitting that a colossal private fortune should be made, as has been urged, out of this work, that supposes success, the very thing desired; for it will be seen by the bill, and your committee have before shown, that no compensation could ever be realized, except as a *consequence* of the fulfillment of all the conditions of the bill, and with a *surplus* created by the work itself. But suppose a great fortune should be acquired: who is wronged by it? And are not the nation and the world benefited? Or, Mr. Whitney may come out *minus*: who will indemnify him? He at least runs a risk; and, as your committee believe, the risk is all on his side. The more he makes, the better; for it is a creation of capital, by the application of labor, now unemployed and useless, to a vast wilderness, and will add so much to the wealth of the nation. Even a private fortune thus made is a part of the public fortune, and will soon be merged in it, no longer to be seen as private." *Sen. Repts.* No. 194, *op. cit.*, pp. 6-7.

[14] *H. Rept.* No. 140, 31st Cong., 1st Sess., (583), pp. 37-39; John P. Davis, *Union Pacific Railway* (Chicago: S. C. Griggs, 1894), pp. 21-26.

[15] *Sen. Exec. Docs.* No. 161, 29th Cong., 1st Sess., (473), p. 7.

perfectly willing to see the project undertaken entirely as a government work,[16] or to take it under his own title at whatever remuneration would be offered to him. " If it is feared," he wrote, " that the remuneration will be disproportionate to the extent and importance of the work, then I am ready to relinquish any claim I may have for compensation, and let the people give me anything or nothing, as they please. If they will but allow me to be their instrument to accomplish this great work, it is enough. I ask no more." [17] Davis summed it up well when he said: [18]

The theory on which Asa Whitney acted was that he was simply an agent of the nation for the purpose of accomplishing a national object; he was not projecting a private enterprise, which, on account of incidental advantages to the nation, was deserving of aid and stimulus from the nation—he was projecting a national enterprise, that could only be accomplished through the medium of individual effort, and in his view, when the project should become a fact, the railway would be only a public or national instrument, requiring individual effort and agency in its manipulation and use. . . .

Whitney's attitude was not the only factor which curtailed the " private" aspect of the projected enterprise. The Whitney bill contained a series of provisions that went a long way towards making it a public enterprise. First of all the road was to be built under the supervision of a government commissioner who was to be appointed by the President with the approval of the Senate.[19] Secondly, the land granted to Whitney was to be sold under the direction of the government commissioner. The proceeds of these sales were to go to Whitney in amounts sufficient to cover the cost of a previously completed ten mile section of the road, and only when the government commissioner was fully

[16] Cong. Globe, Append., 31st Cong., 1st Sess., p. 334.
[17] H. Repts. No. 140, op. cit., p. 16.
[18] Davis, Union Pacific Railway, op. cit., p. 66.
[19] Upon taking office the commissioner was to " superintend the interests of the United States in carrying out the objects of this act; he shall see that the road is promptly and properly constructed, that no waste is committed upon the unsold lands, and that the objects and intentions of this act are fairly and properly carried out. That, when the said Whitney shall have, from time to time, completed the ten-miles section of road, as hereinbefore specified by this act . . . then it shall be the duty of said commissioner, and he is hereby authorized, to grant his certificate of satisfaction to the said Whitney that this act has been complied with. . . ." H. Repts. No. 140, op. cit., p. 48.

satisfied that the funds were actually going to cover incurred expenses.[20] Thirdly, and most important, the road was to be a "*perpetual gratuity* to trade and commerce, with no other tax for transport of passengers and merchandise than such tolls as may be necessary to keep the road and its apparatus in working order." [21] The only compensation to Whitney for his service in management would be $4,000 per year.[22] Fourthly, Congress was to retain full power to fix and regulate the tolls both for passengers and freight.[23] Fifthly, if Whitney suspended work on the road for more than a year or failed "to complete any of the sections of said road within the period herein specified, without good and sufficient reasons for such neglect, to be judged of by Congress, the same right is reserved to Congress to revoke the rights and privileges conferred on them. . . ." [24] Finally, Congress reserved the right " to alter or amend this act, as the public interest may require, so far as it can be done without impairing the rights and privileges of said Whitney and his assigns." [25]

Despite its unorthodoxy and its questionable features, the Whitney plan won wide popular support. Until 1850 it dominated all others. Seventeen state legislatures, large numbers of merchants and businessmen, the press and several Congressional committees put their stamp of approval on it.[26] From one point of view the Whitney plan could not fail to be popular. It offered to give Congress and the country the best of all worlds. The railroad built under the Whitney plan was to be " a work for the benefit of all the great interests of the country, without taxing any of these interests for the construction of it." [27] It was to be privately built, owned and operated but run without profit.

[20] *Ibid.*, pp. 44-46.
[21] *Sen. Repts.* No. 194, *op. cit.*, p. 2.
[22] *H. Repts.* No. 140, *op. cit.*, p. 47.
[23] *Ibid.*
[24] *Ibid.*, p. 50. Haney (*op. cit.*, I, pp. 248-49) holds that, in the case of forfeiture, the bill would have given Whitney those sections of the railroad that were completed at the time of forfeiture. Haney may have based his position on a charge to that effect made by Rep. Bowlin (*Cong. Globe, Append..*, 31st Cong., 1st Sess., p. 332). However there is no such provision in the bill or in any of Whitney's memorials (*H. Repts.* No. 140, *op. cit.*) and Rep. Robinson specifically denied Bowlin's charge. *Cong. Globe, Append.*, 31st Cong., 1st Sess., p. 336.
[25] *H. Repts.* No. 140, *op. cit.*, p. 50.
[26] *H. Repts.* No. 733, 30th Cong., 1st Sess., (526), pp. 16-17.
[27] *Sen. Exec. Docs.* No. 466, 29th Cong., 1st Sess., (478), p. 8.

Unlike a government work it would be impossible for such a railroad to become an engine of politics; but as in a government work, the government would have full power to set and regulate the rates. Above all the Whitney plan was thought to be a scheme in which, as Representative Robinson put it, " the advantage is all on the side of the Government, while the risk is all on the side of Mr. Whitney." [28]

1852-1860: THE PERSISTENCE OF QUASI-GOVERNMENT ENTERPRISE

If the years during which the Whitney plan was pre-eminent can be said to represent one stage in the evolution of thought on the problem of construction and ownership, the period from the eclipse of the Whitney plan ,to the Curtis bill—1852 to 1860—marks off a second stage. Two main features characterized the latter period. One was the sectional conflict over routes, which became increasingly aggravated as time went on and was the main factor preventing the solid majority that favored government aid for a Pacific road from making its will effective.[29] The other was the relatively wide area of agreement on a method of construction and ownership that existed among proponents of a Pacific road from all geographic sections.

The very different ways in which these dual aspects of the Pacific project affected the course of legislative events was dramatically illustrated by successive speeches made by Senator Alfred Iverson of Georgia during the 35th Congress. In the first the earnest defender of the " peculiar institution " joined with California's Gwin and New York's Seward in vigorously defending the constitutionality and judiciousness of the scheme for mixed enterprise projected in Senate bill No. 65. After outlining the magnificent benefits to be derived from a transcontinental road he went on to justify government intervention on the grounds " that without the aid of Government no Pacific

[28] *Cong. Globe, Append.*, 31st Cong., 1st Sess., p. 335.
[29] As early as February, 1853, Senator Mason acknowledged that those " who are determined to make an appropriation are in the majority." But this majority could be thwarted, he said, by promoting " an internecine war among the friends of the measure " on the question of routes. *Cong. Globe*, 32nd Cong., 2d Sess., pp. 817-18.

railroad can or will be built for half a century." [30] There was relatively little difficulty on this score in finding a basis for intersectional unity. By contrast the second speech was an anguished, defiant oration that brought the sectional division to an angry climax. Reiterating his belief in the constitutionality of the bill, Iverson announced that he would never, and he hoped all other Southern Senators would never, agree " to vote so much land and so much money " as this bill proposed, to build a railroad which would be " created outside of a southern confederacy," and bring to the North alone " the countless millions of commercial benefits." [31]

There is no doubt which of the two issues was the more dramatic. Recounting the repetitious provisions on construction and ownership contained in the major bills of this period—the Gwin bill, the Rusk bill, House bill No. 295, in the 33rd Congress, the Douglas bill, the Weller bill and Senate bill No. 65—produces a rather tedious exposition. Yet this repetitiousness—almost to the point of monotony—is in its own way quite as significant as the more colorful split over routes. It casts much light on how essential government intervention was thought to be and on the ease with which the practical men of the time could rationalize their disregard of high doctrine when that doctrine conflicted with a desired end.

The Gwin bill,[32] introduced early in 1853, while not the first to embody this particular pattern, was the first to become the object of any considerable Congressional debate.[33] In it the senior Senator from California called for the building of a Pacific road by a private company selected through the process of competitive bidding. The prime inducement held out to private enterprise for undertaking the work was a land grant of forty sections per mile all along the line in the territories.[34]

[30] *Cong. Globe*, 35th Cong., 1st Sess., pp. 1581-84.
[31] *Ibid.*, 35th Cong., 2d Sess., pp. 242-44.
[32] All bills discussed in this and subsequent sections are examined only with respect to their provisions for construction, finance and ownership.
[33] The first bill to embody this pattern was authored by Senator Douglas and introduced into the First Session of the Thirty-Second Congress. However, it came too late in the session to be debated. *Cong. Globe*, 32d Cong., 1st Sess., p. 2466.
[34] *Ibid.*, 32d Cong., 2d Sess., p. 282. In certain states—those in which branch lines were to be constructed—the bill set aside only twenty sections per mile.

This amount of land, said Gwin, would be more than enough to compensate the contractors for their effort. Even if the lands sold for an average of $1.25 per acre, which the Senator thought to be a minimum, they would yield an average of $27,700 per mile. Since Gwin estimated the average cost of the road at $20,000 per mile, there would be " $7,700 clear profit, over and above the average estimated cost." [35]

Gwin proposed that the contract be awarded to the company or companies whose bid was most advantageous to the United States by the Secretary of War acting under the direction of the President. The President would locate the road. The contractors were to be required to complete a specified section of the road each year and to complete the whole road within ten years. They would receive four-fifths of the land for each 100 mile section as the section was completed, the remaining one-fifth being held as security until the entire road was finished. The work of construction was to be supervised by the government through the appointment of commissioners who, under the direction of the Secretary of War, would " take all necessary measures to protect the public interest, and to see that the terms of the contract are fully and strictly complied with." If the contractors at any time failed to meet the terms of the contract, the existence of such a breach to be determined by Congress, the road and all of the lands would revert to the government. When complete the road would not belong to the contractors in the ordinary sense of ownership. While the contractors might hold and operate the road for a period of time not exceeding thirty years, at the end of the period they had to surrender the road " with all the appurtenances " to the United States without cost. Furthermore, during the period of time in which they held the road all government freight had to be carried free of charge, and Congress was to " have the right, under specified and *protective* limitations, to regulate the charge for [all other] freight and passengers." [36]

Boiled down to its essence Gwin's proposition was that private contractors, aided by a government subsidy, build a road which at the end of three decades would become the property of the government. This basic pattern of private con-

[35] *Ibid.*   [36] *Ibid.*

struction under government supervision and then surrender to the government was the heart of every subsequent bill which received any amount of attention, except the Brooke amendment, during the period designated. The changes made from bill to bill revolved largely around the size of the land grant to be offered and the size or form of any monetary assistance that might be extended. Down to 1860 the leading bills that followed Gwin's were primarily variations on a theme.

The Rusk bill made five pertinent changes in the sections on construction and ownership. Two dealt with the form and amount of government aid: the land grant was reduced from forty to twelve sections per mile in the territories and a provision was added which called on the government to lend the contractors $20,000,000 in five percent United States bonds, redeemable in fifty years. The third change was one which enhanced government control. It stipulated that the company had to keep its books open for the inspection of the President, the Secretary of the Treasury and members of Congress at all times and had to submit annual reports to the government which presented " minutely and in detail the operations of the year preceding." Two of the changes did, however, weaken the governmental element: in one, government control over rates was relaxed by a provision stating that the company's profits could not be reduced below eight percent on the investment, net of the government contribution. In the other, the surrender of the road was put on a compensated basis. The right to require surrender was reserved to Congress, provided the United States paid the contractors an amount of money ten percent greater than their net investment.[37]

When Congressman McDougall introduced House bill No. 295, he was careful to emphasize that the government had " nothing to do " with the road itself " either as a proprietor or director " and that the " location, control and management " was being " left to private enterprise, or to those who by advancing capital, thereby entitle themselves to control its results." [38] Despite these protestations, however, the bill was

[37] *Ibid.*, pp. 469-70. This restriction on the surrender of the road significantly modified the character of the enterprise projected in the Rusk bill and made it less like a government road than any of the other measures that held the center of the stage during the period.

[38] *Cong. Globe, Append.*, 33d Cong., 1st Sess., p. 862.

modeled on the Gwin pattern and, in one respect at least, was considerably more of a proposal for a government road than was the Rusk bill. It reintroduced the concept of mandatory, cost-free surrender, although no final date for such surrender was set. The date was now to be determined in the competitive bidding, with the government presumably favoring, all other things being equal, the company which would hold the road for the shortest period. The Rusk provision for a government loan was dropped, making the only direct aid a land grant of twenty sections per mile. At the same time House bill 295 broke with the free-from-any-toll provisions for government freight and offered to pay up to $600 per mile per year for twenty-five years, the exact amount also to be determined by the competitive bidding.[39] As one of the critics of the bill pointed out, assuming a line 2,000 miles long, this would be equivalent to an annual grant of $1,200,000 or of $30,000,000 in twenty five years.[40] Another innovation, aimed at undercutting the danger of a land monopoly, was the clause which required the company to sell half of the lands granted to it within five years and the rest within ten years. The only major step away from government intervention was the apparent dropping of the provision giving the government the right to regulate freight and passenger rates.[41]

The changes in the Douglas and Weller bills were relatively minor.[42] In the former the land grant was reduced to twelve sections per mile; payment for carrying government mail was cut in half; and a provision requiring contractors to deposit $500,000 as a completion bond was added.[43] In the latter there was only one notable change over the previous bill. That was the re-introduction of a government loan. This one was to be for $2,500,000 in six percent bonds for each one hundred miles of road completed and put into operation to an amount not

[39] Ibid., pp. 862-63, 881-82.
[40] Rep. Perkins, ibid., p. 882.
[41] No such provision is mentioned in the description of the bill. Ibid., pp. 862-63, 881-82.
[42] Bancroft incorrectly attributes the Douglas bill to Gwin. In doing so he calls the bill an impossible measure and unjustly implies that Gwin was spuriously motivated. Works of Hubert Howe Bancroft, XXIV: History of California (San Francisco: History, 1890) VII, pp. 524-26; cf. Russel, op. cit., pp. 191-92.
[43] Cong. Globe, 33d Cong., 2d Sess., p. 749.

exceeding $15,000,000. This loan was to be a first mortgage on the road.[44]

Senate bill No. 65 was pillorized by Davis for being " of the distinctly ' equality of opportunity,' individualistic, *laissez-faire* pattern " and labeled a " fruit of the fungus growth of the theory of ' non-intervention' and ' popular sovereignty.' " Davis grounded his attack on the contention that the only inducement the bill offered potential contractors was the promise of government patronage to add to the gross earnings of the road.[45] In actual fact, however, the aid offered in the bill, far from being niggardly, was actually greater than what had been proposed in any bill previously introduced. The proposed land grant was twenty sections per mile—the same as in House bill 295 and more than was proposed in the Rusk, Weller or Douglas bills. The payment for carrying government freight was to be $500 per mile per year for the mails plus an additional amount for other government freight. In addition the bill proposed to give what was in effect a $25,000,000 loan of five percent bonds to be issued to the contractors at rates of $12,500 per mile as each twenty-five miles of line was completed. However, in order to circumvent earlier constitutional objections to any form of monetary aid, even in the form of a loan, these advances were to be extended as pre-payment on a contract between the government and the company for the carriage of government freight. Besides its liberal provisions on aid, the " most *laissez-faire* " of all the bills included the by then standard provisions for unconditional sale of the land within ten years, posting a $500,000 security bond, forfeiture in case of non-fulfillment of contract, and mandatory, cost-free surrender of the road to the government.[46]

How much these proposals for " private enterprise " resembled a government project can be seen by comparing them to the Wilson amendment which frankly advocated a government built and owned road.[47] The first of four key aspects of the Wilson amendment was a provision directing the President to establish

[44] *Ibid.*, 34th Cong., 1st Sess., pp. 962-63; *Cong. Globe, Append.*, 34th Cong., 1st Sess., p. 477.
[45] Davis, *Union Pacific Railway, op. cit.*, pp. 78-80.
[46] *Cong. Globe*, 35th Cong., 1st Sess., p. 1535.
[47] *Cong. Globe*, 35th Cong., 2d Sess., pp. 577-78.

a board of commissioners composed of five civil engineers who would, subject to the approval of the President, determine the location of the road. Yet far from being novel this same authority was explicitly contained in the Rusk bill which authorized the President " to employ such military officers and troops as he may deem necessary, and also such civil engineers, not exceeding ten in number," [48] and was implicit in every other bill that vested in the President the right to locate the line. Secondly, like all of the previous bills the Wilson amendment provided that the actual work of construction would be done by private companies. A government road did not mean that the road would be constructed by the government itself through engineers, technicians and laborers who were directly on the government payroll. The idea of such a mid-nineteenth century W.P.A. was hardly considered.[49] The only significant difference from previous bills was the provision making the competitive bidding apply to each twenty-five mile section rather than to the line as a whole. Thirdly, like the Rusk and Gwin bills, a specific supervisory body was to be set up to direct the work and let the contracts. But this time instead of the responsibility resting with commissioners working under the Secretary of War (Gwin bill) or engineers working directly under the President (Rusk bill), the supervisory body was to be composed of the Secretary of War, Secretary of Interior, Postmaster General and Attorney General.

What then was it that set the Wilson government road proposal apart from the proposals of Gwin, Douglas, Weller, *et al*? The primary difference was in the method of payment to the private contractors who would actually do the work. For in effect what Gwin and the others were offering these contractors was not the ownership of the road but a unique method of

[48] *Ibid.*, 32d Cong., 2d Sess., p. 469.
[49] In 1865 the *American Railroad Journal* supported a plan which urged that " two or three hundred thousand men " (ex-soldiers) be employed under military discipline for the purpose of building the Pacific railroad. These men were " to receive the usual pay and rations, and to be led by the Engineers of the army." After the road was completed they were to receive " adequate grants of land along the line." The plan was apparently inspired, at least in part, by the increase in unemployment accompanying the end of the Civil War and the demobilization of the army. *Amer. R. R. Jour.*, XXXVIII (April 15 and September 16, 1865), pp. 345-46, 891-92.

paying them for their services and their capital. According to the Wilson bill the contractors would be paid a fixed sum of money directly from the treasury. Under these circumstances, as far as the contractors were concerned, there would be little risk of loss and no opportunity of making great speculative gains. According to the other proposals instead of receiving a specific payment for specific work done, the reward of the contractors was to be of an indefinite amount depending on their own skill, enterprise, shrewdness and luck. In a sense it was a proposal for payment in kind, one part of the payment being the land grant and the other a right—the right to profit from the operation of the railroad for a certain number of years.

To some congressmen the delicate line drawn between the proposals for a " private enterprise " and those which called for a government work was too fine both for their eyesight and their scruples. " It appears to me," said Representative Charles Skelton of New Jersey, " most strange and ridiculous to find statesmen here proposing to build a road from Government funds and Government domain, under the superintendence of Government officers, and yet denying that it will be a governmental work." [50] If it is not a government work, queried a second legislator, " what sort of road will it be " when " it and its appurtenances are transferred to the United States? " [51] " It is a Government work," declared still another with an air of finality. " Its head may be divided, but its body, its legs, its sinews, are of Government. If its beginning may be both in and outside of the Government, its ending will be as surely in it. We have here, plain, clear, indisputably, the *authority* of Congress, the *direction* of Congress, [the] *means* furnished by Congress, to construct these roads." [52]

THE DOMINANCE OF PRAGMATISM

The Congressional penchant for mixed enterprise cannot be explained on doctrinal grounds. If doctrinal views had been pre-eminent, the road would not have been built in the 1860's. The weight of doctrine was on the side of those who, like

[50] *Cong. Globe*, 33d Cong., 2d Sess., p. 280.
[51] Rep. Perkins, *Cong. Globe, Append.*, 33d Cong., 1st Sess., p. 882.
[52] Rep. Hamilton, *ibid.*, 33d Cong., 2d Sess., p. 129.

Representative Garrit Smith, believed "that if it [the railroad] cannot be built unless government build it, then it manifestly should not be built. For if sharp-sighted individual enterprise cannot be tempted to undertake it, then it certainly would be a most unprofitable and unwise undertaking for Government." [53]

But the debate was never really conducted on the doctrinal level. Congress was not beset by two sharply opposed ideologies. The theoretical view which fathered Smith's condemnation was never directly contradicted. Proponents of premature enterprise simply denied the contention that they were projecting anything but a private enterprise. "It is a private enterprise," said McDougall of House bill 295, "aided by the Government, with a stipulation of forfeiture to the Government in case of non-completion of the work." [54] Others ignored the theoretical question, basing the defense of their position on purely pragmatic grounds. For Gwin all that was necessary to justify the project was a cataloguing of the practical benefits that would flow from it in the form of government economies, enhanced trade, new opportunities for the exploitation of natural resources and a more favorable posture in international economic competition. [55]

Those who favored mixed enterprise were not advocates of socialism or even socialistically inclined. They all agreed that profit motivated private enterprise was the most efficient and desirable instrument for economic development and management. Henry Wilson, who from the late fifties on was the leading advocate of a wholly government road, spoke not in the name of Massachusetts' industrial proletariat but in behalf of a "great manufacturing and commercial section, where capital and business centers." [56] Indeed it was not against but in the name of private enterprise and of American commercial supremacy that governmental intervention was urged. It was to the imperial spirit that Gwin ultimately appealed for the passage of S. 65. In a speech foreshadowing an epoch of American development that was still half a century away he declared: [57]

---

[53] *Ibid.*, 33d Cong., 1st Sess., p. 826.
[54] *Cong. Globe*, 33d Cong., 2d Sess., p. 280.
[55] *Ibid.*, 35th Cong., 2d Sess., pp. 53-56.
[56] *Ibid.*, 35th Cong., 1st Sess., p. 1643.
[57] *Ibid.*, 35th Cong., 2d Sess., p. 55.

Commerce is power and empire. Its conquests are greater, more universal and enduring, than those of arms. . . . Give us, as this railroad would, the permanent control of the commerce and exchanges of the world, and in the progress of time and the advance of civilization, we would command the institutions of the world—not like the colonies of Rome, by the sword and vassalage, but by that irresistible moral power which would ultimately carry our institutions with our commerce throughout the sphere we inhabit.

Either England or the United States must in the end control that commerce. It must center in London, Calcutta, and Bombay, or in American cities. It must command the ocean and the land; and we must be secondary to England, or England to America. . . . We have not a day or an hour to lose, if we would secure the great prize of universal commerce. Shall we, the great Power on this continent, stretching soon, with continuous States, from ocean to ocean, step back from our destiny, or wait until England shall have secured the monopoly of this commerce for herself? Is this a British Parliament, or is it a Congress of American statesmen and patriots to whom such an appeal shall be made in vain?

Congressional willingness to entertain the various proposals for mixed enterprise, given agreement on the desirability of a Pacific road, rested on the elemental and indisputable proposition that the early building could not be undertaken except on the basis of government intervention. So obvious was this point that throughout the whole period only Benton, in a 180 degree reversal of his earlier position,[58] actually argued that private enterprise would immediately build the road without land grants, " gifts of money," or any other aid except " the right of way, and payment for transportation of mails, troops, and munitions." [59] But Benton's line of reasoning was tissue-thin and easily brushed aside by McDougall who ridiculed his claim to have found a group of " solid men " ready to undertake the work on this basis. Benton's whole case, said the Californian, was built on nothing more than expressions of interest which lacked " even the weight of a promise." [60]

Nor was it much more difficult to overcome the arguments of those who held that if unaided private enterprise was not immediately ready to build the road, it was " merely a question of

[58] Benton had earlier urged a government road as the only feasible method of construction and ownership. *Ibid.*, 30th Cong., 2d Sess., p. 472.

[59] *Cong. Globe, Append.*, 33d Cong., 2d Sess., p. 73.

[60] *Ibid.*, p. 149.

time " before they would be.[61] Not for fifty years, replied Senator Iverson, not until " the vast country between the present inhabited portions of the United States on the east and west " was settled and developed would "individual wealth and enterprise be bold enough to run the iron horse between the Atlantic and Pacific oceans over any route in the United States. The important, pressing, and controlling exigencies of the Federal Government and the people of the country cannot wait upon so slow a process. Time is important. The demands of public service are pressing. The great interests of commerce, of civilization and of progress, are calling loudly and sharply for action." [62]

While conditions of premature enterprise made governmental intervention inevitable, they did not necessarily dictate the type of intervention which would have to take place. The main proposals of the period need not have been ones in which the governmental features were predominant. They could well have been modeled more along the lines of the Brooke amendment which called for government grants to a private corporation which was to build, own and operate the road with a minimum of government interference.[63]

It was here that the size and relative proportions of government and private investments became a controlling factor. For obviously the government contribution was to be of staggering dimensions. Gwin had, after all, proposed a land grant of over 150,000 square miles—a territory as large as all of New England plus New York and Pennsylvania.[64] And while S. 65 had reduced the land grant to an area" only " about the size of Ohio, it also called for an advance of $25,000,000. Some experts considered even these grants, gargantuan by all past standards, inadequate. The *American Railroad Journal* commented sarcastically that with offers such as these a person might as well "hope to storm the rock of Gibraltar with cannon loaded with *green peas*, as to construct a railroad to the Pacific." [65] In a speech before the American Geographical Society Henry V. Poor declared that " unless the general govern-

---

[61] See, for example, the speech by Rep. Galusha Grow; *Cong. Globe*, 33d Cong., 2d Sess., p. 290.

[62] *Ibid.*, 35th Cong., 1st Sess., p. 1581.

[63] *Ibid.*, 32d Cong., 2d Sess., p. 315.

[64] *Ibid.*, p. 281.

[65] *Am. R. R. Jour.*, XXVII (June 24, 1854), p. 386.

ment will furnish a considerable portion of the cost, say $50,000 per mile [or $100,000,000 for a road 2,000 miles long], and upon favorable terms, the construction of a road upon any of the routes is out of the question." [66] Pike of Maine went even further, stating that all of the money for the road would eventually have to be put up by the government, that it was self-deception to expect " to get any amount worth reckoning out of private individuals." [67] It was precisely this lack of confidence that led Wilson to advocate a government road. He believed that no businessman would want to invest in the Pacific railroad because " every dollar invested in making such a road " would be " lost to the stockholders." [68]

Even if forecasts like those of Pike and Wilson could be disregarded as being far too gloomy, one could not deny nor ignore the fact that the government's contribution would be more than an incidental subsidy or an additional incentive for the carrying through of a project in which the lion's share of the cost was being borne by private individuals. This was the fact that apparently impelled Congress towards a government relationship that was more than casual. In the light of the size and proportion of the expected public contribution, various controls and a stipulation for surrender after a given number of years seemed reasonable. Representative John G. Davis of Indiana, who categorically rejected the idea of a government built road, viewed the question of surrender to the government after the completion of the line in a different manner. " My present impression," he said, " is, that this matter should be reserved, or, at least, not placed entirely beyond the future control of Congress." [69]

At least three other factors also spurred the tendency toward greater rather than less government intervention. One was the widespread concern over the danger of a monopoly, especially if only one road were built. It was on this danger that Gwin played when he attacked the Brooke amendment as a scheme to " create a gigantic monopoly with more power than the great East India Company, and infinitely greater than the Bank of

---

[66] *Ibid.*, (June 3, 1854), p. 342.
[67] *Cong. Globe*, 37th Cong., 2d Sess., p. 1707.
[68] *Ibid.*, 35th Cong., 1st Sess., p. 1644.
[69] *Cong. Globe, Append.*, 33d Cong., 1st Sess., p. 964.

the United States ever possessed." Centering his fire on the fact that all government controls over rates would cease once the loan to the government was repaid, Gwin argued that there was no end to the " exorbitant extraction " that would be made against both private individuals and government if they were left " entirely at the mercy of the company." [70]

The second was the fear that the project might fall into the hands of speculators whose object would be to make a killing rather than to build a road. This fear of stockjobbing, as well as of the possibilities of wasteful extravagances and other shady dealings, was all the more aggravated by the knowledge that those who undertook the project would be working largely with money other than their own.

Finally, a high degree of government intervention was less obnoxious than it might otherwise have been because railroads in general, and this one in particular, stood in many ways in a category apart from all other types of business enterprise. Railroads were thought to be " the great instrument of land commerce and trade " whose superiority to all other forms of transportation made them absolutely indispensable for economic growth and survival in economic competition.[71] In the expanding market economy of the times all other forms of business were dependent on them. In other words railroads were thought to have a public character not possessed by other types of enterprise. If for many American communities this had been reason enough for government intervention in local railway projects, how much more justification there was for subordinating theory to the exigencies of practical life and adopting a special attitude in the case of the first transcontinental railroad. There was " no doubt," said one writer with reference to the Pacific project, " that the ideal principle of democratic progress demands the absolute non-interference of Government in all enterprises whose benefit accrues to a part of its citizens, or which can be stimulated into life by the spontaneous operation of popular interest. But facts are not ideal, and absolute principles in their practical application make head only by a curved line of compromise with the facts." [72]

[70] Cong. Globe, 32d Cong., 2d Sess., pp. 315-16.
[71] J. W. Scott, op. cit., p. 564.
[72] Fitz-Hugh Ludlow, " Through-tickets to San Francisco: A Prophecy," Atlantic Monthly, XIV (November, 1864), pp. 605-06.

TOWARD AN ECLECTIC CONCLUSION

The Curtis bill marks the beginning of the third and final stage in the evolution of thought on a Pacific road. Russel offers the opinion that the plan of financing put forward in this bill "showed that speculative investors were finally beginning to gather about the flesh pots." [73] An even stronger charge was made at the time of the bill's introduction by Representative John H. Reagan. The Texas legislator implied that Congress was being swayed by lobbyists who wanted a bill easily vulnerable to dishonest manipulations. These individuals, he said, would never "touch the enterprise" if they were "limited to just and honest profits on the capital invested." [74] How much truth there was to this charge is difficult to ascertain. Aside from Reagan's statement there is no direct evidence of the influence of speculators on the bent of Congress.

But it is not the puzzzle of the link between the Curtis bill and speculators which makes the former a major landmark in the procession of proposals on a Pacific road. The Curtis bill is entitled to that eminence because it represented a definite shift in emphasis on the problem of finance and ownership—a conscious movement away from the type of scheme that dominated the previous period. The new feature of this bill was not opposition to government aid. It advocated a larger largess than those envisioned in most of the major bills of the past. Progenitor of the Act of 1862, its salient feature was its advocacy of a freer hand for private enterprise. For whatever reasons, the Curtis bill reflected a new and strong trend in Congress for accommodation to the wishes of private capital despite the increased danger to the public interest which such accommodation might entail.

The report of the Select Committee that framed the bill sheds little light on the motives for this shift in emphasis. It states only that there was "the greatest diversity of opinion" as to methods of construction and that the plan adopted was the one favored by a majority. [75] To this bland statement Curtis later added the remark that the committee sought a plan by which

[73] Russel, *op. cit.*, p. 283.
[74] *Cong. Globe*, 36th Cong., 1st Sess., p. 2337.
[75] *H. Repts.* No. 428, 36th Cong., 1st Sess., (1069), pp. 16-18.

the government would " do just as much as " was " necessary, and no more." [76]

Of course, the claim that the government's role was to be limited to a minimum was not new. It had been the expedient preface to every previous bill introduced no matter how heavily weighted to the government side, except those which avowedly advocated a public enterprise. In this case, however, there was substance to the claim. The Curtis bill called on the government to advance a loan of $60,000,000 in the form of thirty year, five percent United States bonds.[77] This aid was expected to account for approximately one-half of the cost of construction. Responsibility for the work was to be vested in a group of selected individuals who were to control construction and own the road. While it was expected that these individuals would organize a corporation with stock subscriptions open to the public, no specific provision to that effect was made in the bill. Even if such a corporation were formed, the bill was so drawn that control over the enterprise could be kept wholly in the hands of the original group instead of being invested in the stockholders. Furthermore, earlier provisions intended to secure the public stake in the road, such as government supervision of construction and surrender of the line after a stated period of time, were dispensed with. Thus the Curtis bill asked Congress to give a group of individuals a larger loan than had been contemplated in earlier bills while tending, at the same time, to substitute reliance on the good faith of promoters for specific controls.[78]

The new emphasis on a freer hand for private enterprise did not go uncontested. The old penchant for heavy government controls still had deep roots among the legislators. The Curtis plan came under heavy criticism in the 36th Congress.[79] But it was especially in the 37th Congress, during the debates immediately leading up to the passage of the Act of 1862, that the conflict between these two tendencies was most marked. Two instances illustrate the clash. In the first, the House added five

[76] *Cong. Globe*, 36th Cong., 1st Sess., p. 2332.

[77] In addition there was to be a land grant of one alternate section per mile. *Ibid.*, p. 2333; *H. Repts.* No. 428, *op. cit.*, p. 16.

[78] *Cong. Globe*, 36th Cong., 1st Sess., pp. 2332-37, 2411-19, 2448-52.

[79] *Ibid.*

government representatives to the board of commissioners [80] and two to the board of directors of the Union Pacific company, thus overriding the objections of those who wanted management of the company to rest exclusively with private capital without any interference from " irresponsible agents whom the government may appoint." [81]   In the second, the Senate, believing that the creation of a " mammoth monopoly to run on forever" without any power to control it " would be monstrous," insisted on a provision giving Congress the right to amend or repeal the act in the future.[82]

Such victories for tighter government controls did not, however, turn the clock back to the pre-Curtis era. The Act of 1862 was not a plan for a government enterprise, or like the Gwin bill, a close approximation of it. There was no doubt to whom the road belonged. The provision for two government directors on a board of fifteen did not shift control of the company from private capital to the government. It was a small enough concession to make to those who favored a government road or some provision for eventual surrender to the government.

If the Act of 1862 was not a plan for a government work, neither was it a carte blanche to private enterprise. The promoters of the road still had to suffer the surveillance of government commissioners whose approval of the work of construction on each forty mile section was necessary before they received a single dollar of government money or a single acre of land.[83] And, even though a given section was approved by the commissioners, one-fourth of all of the bonds to which the company was entitled would still remain with the government as a security against the full completion of the road. If the road was not completed, not only the bonds held on reserve but the

[80] The board of commissioners was the body empowered to organize the corporation.

[81] *Ibid.*, 37th Cong., 2d Sess., pp. 1890-91.

[82] *Ibid.*, pp. 2779-80.

[83] The Act of 1862 awarded the Union Pacific a land grant of ten sections per mile plus a loan of thirty year, six percent United States bonds. The bonds were to be given to the company at the rate of $16,000 for each mile of line from the Eastern end of the line to the Rocky Mountains, $48,000 per mile for the next 150 miles, $32,000 per mile until the base of the Sierra Nevada Mountains, then $48,000 for another 150 miles, and then $16,000 a mile until San Francisco. The maximum amount of the loan was set at $50,000,000. *Cong. Globe, Append.*, 37th Cong., 2d Sess., pp. 382-83.

entire line with all of its appurtenances would be forfeited to the government. In addition, while the Act did not give Congress the unrestricted right to control rates, it did permit them to reduce rates if the net earnings of the company exceeded ten percent of the cost of the road. Finally there was that " pernicious " proviso giving Congress the right, at any time, to " add to, alter, amend or repeal " the act, a proviso which, when enforced sixteen years later, was attacked by Henry Poor as " a gross and unwarranted assumption of power " and an invitation to " a despotism of caprice or passion, or something worse." [84]

Thus, Congress did not completely break with the past. What it approved was still basically a plan for mixed enterprise. Unlike the schemes of the earlier period, however, it was now the private elements in the bill that predominated. The Act of 1862 was a measure of expediency which sought to speed up the natural course of economic development under private enterprise while at the same time avoiding the extreme of government, or quasi-government, enterprise. It was the eclectic product of two opposing tendencies. What Congress did was to mock the ways of the experimental agriculturalists and, by hot house methods, attempt to mature the project for a transcontinental road artificially—to artificially make it subject to profitable private investment.

Congress' hot house hybrid was not quite as attractive to the promoters of the railroad as it was to its originators. As McDougall intimated, regardless of what Congress thought of the Act it was the men who built railroads who would have to render the ultimate judgement.[85] And these men called the Act inadequate. At first criticism was directed mainly against such provisions as the requirement that one-fourth of the government bonds be reserved until the road was completed. But by the time the 38th Congress opened, the group which had gained control of the Union Pacific was asking for much more than the repeal of a few restrictive provisions. They could not, they asserted, build the road without greatly in-

[84] *Ibid.*, pp. 381-84; Henry V. Poor, " The Pacific Railroad," *North American Review*, CXXXVIII (July, 1879), p. 680.
[85] *Cong. Globe*, 37th Cong., 3d Sess., pp. 1245-46.

creased aid from the government. Their request was that the government subsidy be doubled.[86]

This demand provoked a burst of antagonism. Those who viewed even the Act of 1862 as a great give-away, regarded this new appeal as an expression of unrestrained rapaciousness. Representative Holman of Indiana belittled the motives of the promoters and urged Congress to drive a hard bargain with them. " The patriotism of this thing does not weigh a feather in the estimation of these people," he said. It was only a " question of dollars and cents " with them, only " a question of capital and revenue." [87] To Representative Washburne the whole thing was a crude attempt to raid the government treasury and nothing more. It deserved only to be rebuffed.[88]

The most interesting position was the one taken by John V. L. Pruyn of New York, who had been working very closely with the company and was himself one of its stockholders. Representative Pruyn proposed that the charter of the company be revoked and the road be built by the government through a board of commissioners. Shunning attacks on the personal honesty of the promoters, his reasoning was simple and straightforward: the government was putting up $100,000,000, and private capital only two percent of that amount. In other words, he said, the government was in fact building the road and therefore ought to own it. He had no objection " to an organization which, by contributing a proper amount for this purpose, would really, in view of the hazard it incurs, become entitled to something." But such was not the case. To the objection that construction by the government would lead to waste, corruption and inefficiency Pruyn replied: " I do believe the road could be built by the Government under the supervision of such men as I would have appointed—men outside of all political connection with the Government, and of high standing and character—not only cheaper, but better and more useful for the great purpose for which the road is to be constructed, than any company would be likely to build it, because they would have in view all the great elements of durability and useful-

---

[86] *Am. R. R. Jour.*, XXXV (September 13, 1862), pp. 705, 719-22; *Cong. Globe*, 38th Cong., 1st Sess., p. 3155; and 37th Cong., 3d Sess., pp. 1245-46.

[87] *Ibid.*, 38th Cong., 1st Sess., pp. 3022-23.

[88] *Ibid.*, pp. 3150-52.

ness which should belong to a great national work of this kind. . . ."[89]

Congress rejected Pruyn's plan for a government road[90] as they did another of his proposals which aimed at preventing some of the chicanery that later followed.[91] The majority of Congress felt that further inducements for the work were in order. Consequently while unwilling to vote the company any more money, they agreed to reduce the government lien to a second mortgage and to permit the company to issue its own first-mortgage bonds.[92] They also increased the land grant to twenty sections per mile and repealed the provision which required twenty-five percent of the government bonds to be held in reserve.[93]

Thus the Act of 1864 represented a further step in the direction of accommodation to private capital. While the amount of money which the government was to extend was not increased, the amount which the promoters of the road would have to invest was greatly reduced. It was a critical decision. It opened the way for the huge profits that later followed. Nevertheless, it did not eliminate the quality of mixed enterprise. Aside from the subordination of the government lien the only weakening of government control was the repeal of the provision for a reserve. And this was counterbalanced by the increase in the number of government directors from two out of fifteen to five out of twenty.[94] The idea of a partnership between the government and private capital was retained.

[89] *Ibid.*, pp. 3149-50, 3181-82.

[90] The vote was 72 to 20. *Ibid.*, p. 3244.

[91] Pruyn proposed that before any bonds were issued the Secretary of the Treasury examine all construction contracts to verify that they were "fair and *bona fide*" and in the interest of the company and the United States. *Ibid.*

[92] The first-mortgage bonds issued by the company could not exceed the amount of bonds loaned to the company by the United States. *Cong. Globe, Append.*, 38th Cong., 1st Sess., p. 251.

[93] *Ibid.*, pp. 250-51.

[94] *Ibid.*, p. 251.

CHAPTER III

THE DOUBLE IRONY OF THE ACTS
OF 1862 AND 1864 [1]

*Under one name or another a ring of some seventy persons is struck,
at whatever point the Union Pacific is approached. As stockholders
they own the road, as mortgagees they have a lien upon it, as directors
they contract for its construction, and as members of the Credit
Mobilier they build it.*

Charles Francis Adams, Jr.

The Acts of 1862 and 1864 were written by men striving to
avoid the profligacy they associated with government enterprise.
These legislators wanted to take only the minimum steps
necessary to induce responsible businessmen to embark on the
building of the Pacific road. The 20,000,000 acre land grant
and the projected loan of $60,000,000 were expected to provide
about half the capital necessary for construction; the rest was
to come from private parties. It was to the self-interest of the
individuals who were expected to invest at least $50,000,000
that the legislators looked for the dynamic force that would
insure rapid construction at minimum cost.[2]

Judged solely on the basis of the speed of construction and
the technical soundness of the Union Pacific, the Acts of 1862
and 1864 were extremely efficacious. There were, it was true,
certain deficiencies in the road. Some embankments were too
shallow; at some points the ballasting was too light; certain

[1] The following notation will be used in this chapter and the next one:
   Wilson—for U. S. Congress, House, *Affairs of the Union Pacific Railroad
      Company*, 42d Cong., 3d Sess., Rept. No. 78 (1577).
   Poland—for U. S. Congress, House, *Credit Mobilier Investigation*, 42d
      Cong., 3d Sess., Rept. No. 77, (1577).
   PRC   —for U. S. Congress, Senate, *Testimony Taken by the United States
      Pacific Railway Commission*, 50th Cong., 1st Sess., Exec. Docs. No.
      51, 8 Vols. (2505-2509).

[2] *Cong. Globe*, 37th Cong., 2d Sess., p. 2788. Representative James H. Campbell, chairman of the House committee on the Pacific road, estimated that the
road would cost an average of $60,000 per mile. Congress proposed to loan the
builders an average of $29,000 per mile. *Ibid.*, pp. 1579, 1707.

51

curves were too sharp. But such deficiencies were, " almost without exception, incident to new roads " or related to the " peculiar difficulties " under which this road had been built.[3] They were not serious enough to detract from the overall quality of the work. The road was " equal, in all respects, to the best of our first-class Eastern roads, and superior to most of them," reported a civil engineer sent to examine the line for Jay Cooke.[4] A similar reconnaissance led the editor of the *Philadelphia Bulletin* to comment: " Everything indicates a determination that the work now done shall be as durable as human ingenuity and enterprise can make it. The workshops, engine houses and other structures at Omaha, Cheyenne, North Platte and Laramie, are all handsome stone and brick edifices, that will last without repair or reconstruction for generations; while the road itself is as solidly and substantially built as any railroad in America." [5] From an engineering point of view, the achievement was all the more remarkable in the light of the fact that the road was completed in only five years. " The energy exhibited in prosecuting this work," said the editors of the *Commercial and Financial Chronicle*, " is beyond all precedent, and reflects the greatest credit on the management under whom the company's affairs are conducted." [6]

This high praise of the engineering accomplishments of the promoters was, however, soon drowned in a louder and more persistent chorus of criticism. In January of 1869, Philadelph Van Trump, a Representative from Ohio, took the floor of Congress to give public voice to what had previously been common rumor. The promoters of the road, he charged, were engaged in " gigantic schemes of public plunder." They had combined to form a construction company (the Credit Mobilier) the interests of which were adverse to the interests of the Union Pacific. They had created " a situation so delicate and so full of temptation . . . that no honest man or men would desire " to be in their position. The exact amount of their plunder was not known since " the actual cost of the road to the contracting

[3] U. S. Congress, House, *Report of the Secretary of Interior, 1868*, 40th Cong., 3d Sess., Exec. Docs. No. 1 (1366), p. xii.

[4] *Am. R. R. Jour.*, XLII (July 24, 1869), p. 817.

[5] *Am. R. R. Jour.*, XLI (August 22, 1868), p. 817.

[6] *Commercial and Financial Chronicle*, III (August 25, 1866), p. 248.

company is shown only by their private books," but to Van Trump's mind there was no doubt that these men were "engaged in a specimen of the ' confidence game '." [7] From time to time the accusation was reiterated in Congress and in the press. But it was not until the *New York Sun*, in the heat of the election campaign of 1872, accused the promoters of the Union Pacific of having bribed the Vice-President, the Secretary of the Treasury, the Speaker of the House and 12 other members of Congress that the affairs of the Union Pacific and the Credit Mobiler became a *cause célèbre*.[8]

The House established two committees to investigate these allegations. The Poland committee found enough evidence of bribery to recommend the expulsion of two members of the House.[9] The Wilson committee, which concentrated on the financial affairs of the Credit Mobilier, concluded that the promoters had made profits of at least $23,000,000 on a personal investment of less than $4,000,000; that these enormous profits could by no means be justified as a reward for risk bearing since the risk "was wholly that of the government" whose credit had secured the bulk of the capital necessary for construction; that the completed road was saddled with a capitalization more than twice the actual cost of construction and a debt which equalled or exceeded the entire value of the road's property; that the Union Pacific was "weak," "poor," and "kept from bankruptcy only by the voluntary aid of a few capitalists." [10]

Thus, what Horace Greeley had proclaimed the " grandest and noblest enterprise of our age " [3] was transformed into an object of national shame. It was ironic, indeed, that Congress in shunning a government enterprise as an invitation to profligacy should have instead spawned the Credit Mobilier scandal. To the investigators of 1873 this twist of fate was entirely attributable to the dishonesty of the men to whom the work had been entrusted. The Union Pacific was in a state of near prostration because it had been built by a group of men who

---

[7] *Cong. Globe*, 40th Cong., 3d Sess., pp. 528-30.
[8] Rhodes, VII, *op. cit.*, p. 1.
[9] Poland, pp. XVIII-XIX.
[10] Wilson, pp. XV, XX-XXI.
[11] From a letter printed in the *Am. R. R. Jour.*, XXXVI (June 20, 1863), p. 593.

wantonly disobeyed the " express directions " of Congress, who maliciously abrogated the various safeguards that Congress had put into these enactments. If not for the extortionate extraction of profit, the Union Pacific would have been a " solvent, powerful, well-endowed company able to perform its important public functions without interruption in times of commercial disaster and in times of war," instead of being a company that tottered on the brink of bankruptcy.[12] The verdict of the Wilson committee has, by and large, been accepted by most historians. " The directors of the Union Pacific," write Nevins and Commager, " not content with government largess, organized a dummy construction company and voted that company fraudulent contracts that netted them profits running into millions of dollars," thus saddling the road " with such debts that the government had to whistle for its loans and communities which they served had to pay exorbitant charges for a generation to come." [13]

Close examination raises a number of severe doubts about the validity of the analysis contained in the Wilson report. These doubts do not relate to the committee's characterization of the intentions or the personal integrity of the promoters. The charge that they engaged in profiteering and sought to seduce public officials seems to be well-founded. In at least one respect history has, if anything, probably underestimated the deliberateness with which the promoters acted to inflate their profits.[14] But this demonstration of the moral turbidity of the promoters is, perhaps, the only well-drawn aspect of the Wilson report. The investigators' discussion of the profit on the construction of the road suffers both because their estimate of the amount of the profit is, in all likelihood, overstated and because they did not clearly define the nature of the risk confronting the promoters. If the risk was sufficiently great, the gap between the actual profit and a " reasonable " profit might have been considerably narrower than is implied by the Wilson report.

The most improbable aspect of the analysis presented by the investigators is the contention that the financially precarious

---

[12] Wilson, pp. III-IV, XIX-XXII.

[13] Allan Nevins and Henry Steele Commager, *The Pocket History of the United States* (New York: Pocket Books, 1951), p. 314.

[14] See below, pp. 85-86.

perch of the Union Pacific in 1872 was due to the amount of profit extracted by the promoters. In dealing with this question most previous studies have centered attention on the total capitalization of the Union Pacific. The total capitalization included both the bonded debt and the stock issue of the firm. However, the size of the stock issue *per se* had no bearing on the financial stability of the firm. The solvency of the Union Pacific turned on the company's ability to meet the interest payments on its bonded debt. Hence the size of the stock issue entered into the question of solvency only to the degree that it induced an increase in the amount of debt. In other words, the relevant issue is not the extent to which the profiteering resulted in an inflation of the total capitalization, but the extent to which it inflated the bonded debt. And here the record seems to indicate that the greatest portion (perhaps 85 percent) of the proceeds of the various bonds sales were used to meet necessary construction costs and operating expenses.

The second irony of the Acts of 1862 and 1864, then, is this: Even if the promoters of the Union Pacific had scrupulously limited themselves to the profit justified by the risk they had borne, the attempt to build the road under the provisions of these enactments would still have resulted in a bonded debt which exceeded the cost of construction and in interest charges which amounted to between 113 and 124 percent of the net income of the road in 1872. With respect to the post-construction financial stability of the firm, the great deficiency was not in the character of the promoters but in the character of the enactments.

THE FACTUAL BACKGROUND

The first step in the activization of the corporation chartered by Congress was taken on September 2, 1862. On that day the 163 incorporating commissioners named by Congress met in Chicago.[15] Their task was the organization of a campaign to sell Union Pacific stock. At least $2,000,000 (2,000 shares) had to be subscribed and a ten percent installment paid before a management could be elected.[16] The subscription drive was

[15] The meeting is described in *Am. R. R. Jour.*, XXXV (Sept. 13, 1862), pp. 705, 719-22.

[16] *Cong. Globe, Append.*, 37th Cong., 2d Sess., p. 382.

launched at the Chicago meeting in a spirit of enthusiasm and high optimism. Books were opened in New York, Boston, Chicago and other principal cities and towns of the North and West. Yet despite the fanfare with which the drive was started, despite the patriotic exhortations from prominent citizens, subscriptions were exceedingly slow in coming in. Six months after the Chicago meeting only $300,000 had been pledged "and this chiefly in the far West." The "capitalists of the East," said the *American Railroad Journal*, were waiting for certain amendments "and for an understanding with each other as to the best method of securing success for the project, before entering into the necessary financial arrangement." [17] Toward the end of September, 1863—a full year after the Chicago meeting— the situation had changed so little that even the more sanguine supporters of the Pacific road concluded that "the project had been abandoned." Then, quite unexpectedly, on September 25th, a group of men of " enormous wealth " came forward to supply the necessary amount of capital to launch the enterprise.[18]

With $2,177,000 subscribed and a ten percent installment paid, a stockholders meeting was called for the last week in October.[19] From this meeting there emerged a group of officers and a board of directors. The man elected president was General John A. Dix, a former Secretary of the Treasury. The treasurer of the company was John J. Cisco, a banker and a former assistant Secretary of the Treasury. The vice-president and dominant figure in the enterprise was Thomas C. Durant. A leading railroad man of the time, closely associated with Henry Farnam in the building of the Mississippi and Missouri, Durant was the effective chief executive of the firm. He was the company's general agent as well as its chief fund raiser. He also bore the main responsibility for liaison with Congress and the government. Others included on the first board of directors who figured prominently in later events were C. S. Bushnell, a New York " merchant prince," and H. S. McComb, a leather merchant, whose spectacular charges provided the basis for the *New York Sun* exposé.[20]

---

[17] *Am. R. R. Jour.*, XXXVI (February 28, 1863), p. 189.

[18] *Ibid.*, (October 3, 1863), p. 925.

[19] *Ibid.*, (November 7, 1863), p. 1047.

[20] Edwin L. Sabin, *Building the Pacific Railway* (Philadelphia: J. B. Lippincott, 1919), Chapter III; Wilson, pp. 597-98.

The problem of funds.

The most pressing problem facing the directors of the new company was not the organization of construction but the raising of capital. Engineers had placed the cost of building and equipping the road over the plains between Omaha and the Rocky Mountains at about $27,500 per mile.[21] Since the government bonds were to be issued only as each 40 mile section was completed and approved, the promoters required a minimum of $1,100,000 to begin construction. The building of each succeeding 40 mile section would be partially financed by the government bonds issued on the previous section. If these bonds sold at par, they would account for somewhat less than 60 percent of the cost of construction. Hence, even with the government loan, the promoters faced the task of raising $11,500 for each mile beyond the initial 40. Simply to meet the direct construction charges the company had to raise $1,790,000 for the first 100 miles, $2,940,000 for 200 miles, $4,090,000 for 300, and $7,540,000 to bring the road to the foot of the Rocky Mountains. In addition, funds were needed for engineering surveys, fees and legal expenses, interest payments, administrative charges, and other costs not included in construction estimates.[22] Over and above the government subsidy the promoters had to obtain a total of $12,000,000 to reach the mountains. The $218,000 paid in on Union Pacific stock met the legal requirement for the activization of the charter; but it was hardly enough to get the road five miles out of Omaha.

From October of 1863 to the summer of 1865 the energies of the promoters were primarily directed to the procurement of funds. The most promising source of additional monies was Congress. Durant, Bushnell, McComb and four lawyers were dispatched to Washington to press for a doubling of the government loan. As Bushnell said, they " came early in the session of 1863 and remained throughout that long session almost constantly in attendance." Their " efforts resulted in the legislation of 1864." [23] The demand for increased government credit was rejected. Instead they secured the right to issue their own first-

[21] Wilson, pp. 114, 241, 669, 675.
[22] *Ibid.*, p. 637.
[23] *Ibid.*, p. 39; see also pp. 102-12, 127-29, 173.

mortgage bonds. Congress also provided that the government bonds should be issued at the completion of each 20 miles rather than each 40.[24]

After six months of lobbying the promoters had no more working capital than before. By reducing the mileage required for each allotment of government bonds Congress had, it is true, halved the private capital needed for the initial section. But this was a negative sort of aid. It put no coins into the company's coffers. The first-mortgage bonds were only a potential source of funds. According to the law this security could not be sold until at least 20 miles of track were constructed, and then in amounts not exceeding the government issue.[25] Moreover, the money that could be realized on the first-mortgage bonds depended on the prices at which the market was willing to absorb them. As far as immediately available funds were concerned, the promoters were, if anything, worse off than before since about $250,000 had been expended in the course of the campaign to push the amendment through.[26]

Following the passage of the Act of 1864 attention turned to the possibility of using the company's stock to raise capital. A call was issued for a second installment on the stock that had already been subscribed. This call produced $110,000 in 1864 and $4,000 in the next year.[27] The company then launched a new campaign for stock subscriptions. In the spring of 1865 books were again opened " in the principal cities of the Union," and " expensive advertisements " were published. The results of the second campaign were even more dismal than the first. " Not a dollar was subscribed," said government director Charles T. Sherman. " We considered, therefore, that the idea of building the road by means of subscription of stock was a failure." [28]

The capital needed to begin construction was finally obtained in two ways. First, Durant and seven other men—all directors or stockholders of the Union Pacific—put up $1,400,000.[29] The money was not invested directly in the railroad company. It was

[24] Cong. Globe, Append., 38th Cong., 1st Sess., p. 251.
[25] Ibid.; see also above, pp. 48-50.
[26] Wilson, pp. 102-12, 137, 173-79; Trottman, op. cit., pp. 19-20.
[27] Wilson, pp. 742-43.
[28] Ibid., p. 664.
[29] Ibid., p. 160.

put in the Credit Mobilier, a corporation acquired by Durant for the express purpose of financing the Union Pacific's construction contracts. Funds were shunted from the Credit Mobilier to the railroad through an agreement which called on the construction company to buy $500,000 of Union Pacific stock. The Credit Mobilier also agreed to lend money to the Union Pacific, taking the railroad's first-mortgage bonds as security.[30] Secondly, Durant was able to secure a large short-term loan. Through the aid of John Pondir, a broker introduced to Durant by the Secretary of the Interior, a syndicate of New York banks was organized for the purpose of lending $1,000,000 to the Union Pacific. The loan was consummated in May of 1865. Scrip on the government bonds taken at 90 provided the necessary collateral.[31]

Two million four hundred thousand dollars was enough to start construction, but not enough to sustain it for any considerable distance. After 100 miles, construction would grind to a halt unless new funds could be raised at a rate of about $20,000 per mile. The resources of the original Credit Mobilier investors had been taxed to the limit. Additional funds required the involvement of new adventurers. By drawing 35 new stockholders into the corporation, the Credit Mobilier was able to increase its paid-in capital to $2,000,000 in the summer of 1865, and to $2,500,000 in the spring of the following year.[32] At the same time the Union Pacific resorted to large-scale borrowing of short-term funds. Using the company's first-mortgage bonds as collateral, the railroad obtained as much money in this way as it had from the Credit Mobilier. However, these loans carried with them a rate of interest that varied between one and one and one-half percent *per month*.[33]

By December, 1866, some 305 miles of track had been laid, the capital of the Credit Mobilier had been exhausted and the Union Pacific was three or four million dollars in debt.[34] More money was needed. The promoters sought to obtain it by again increasing the capital stock of the Credit Mobilier. An issue of

[30] Poland, p. 61; Wilson, pp. 64-65.
[31] PRC, I, pp. 437-38; Wilson, pp. 40, 252.
[32] Wilson, pp. 155, 160; Poland, p. 19.
[33] Wilson, pp. 41, 252; cf. Wilson, p. 557 and PRC, V, pp. 3489, 3493.
[34] Sabin, *op. cit.*, p. 147; Poland, p. 179.

$1,250,000 was voted in February. Each stockholder was to be entitled to purchase additional shares equal to one-half of his original holding. Believing that the new offering would be more difficult to market than previous ones, the promoters decided to give prospective investors a free bonus of Union Pacific first-mortgage bonds equal to the amount of their new stock purchase. This expectation proved to be correct. Many "old subscribers could not take their portion of the new stock, and many others thought the thing looked so blue that they would not take it." [35] By July of 1867 the persistent promoters had managed to push sales to just over the million dollar mark.[36] But by July the promoters had also exhausted the proceeds of the sale. A rate of construction that carried the railroad 125 miles closer to the mountains in four months drained the new funds as quickly as they were acquired.[37] A financial crisis more serious than those of the past seemed to be at hand. It never materialized. During the summer of 1867 Bushnell began to sell first-mortgage bonds which until that time had been used only as collateral for loans. Within six months bonds with a face value of $10,000,000 were sold at prices in the neighborhood of 95.[38] The promoters could now obtain all of the funds they needed.

[35] Wilson, pp. 36, 40-41; Poland, p. 179.

[36] Ham's testimony implied that the promoters had sold $1,032,000 of stock by July 15, 1867. Wilson, p. 19.

[37] Sabin, *op. cit.*, p. 155.

[38] Wilson, p. 41. The approximate starting date of Bushnell's campaign can be deduced from the testimony of Bushnell and Ham, and from the ledger on first-mortgage bonds.

The first sales of the bonds listed in the ledger were connected with the 1867 issue of Credit Mobilier stock. Through June 1, the Credit Mobilier needed $957,000 in bonds to meet its commitments on the stock. The ledger shows that this amount of bonds was issued by June 19th. During the balance of June, the Credit Mobilier sold only $5,500 of additional stock. However, $305,000 in bonds were sold during the same period. This would seem to place the start of Bushnell's drive in the last two weeks of June. Bond sales were relatively moderate for the next five months. About 1,000 bonds (with a face value of $1,000 each) were sold in July and again in August. The amount sold dropped to 716 in September and to 672 in October, the month of the Ames contract. In November the sales still hovered about 700, but in December they shot up to 2,450. In January, 1868, 1,944 were sold to the public and in February sales reached 3,240. Wilson, pp. 19, 619-21, 643.

The construction contracts.

Construction could have been organized in either of two main ways. The Union Pacific could have acted as its own general contractor, directly entering into agreements with the sub-contractors who performed the actual work. Alternatively, the railroad could have made its agreements with general contractors who would then have sub-contracted with various parties for grading, track laying, the erection of stations, buildings, etc. The latter method was adopted. The road was built under three contracts. The first was made with a man named H. M. Hoxie. It set the terms for the construction of the first 247 miles. The second was made with Oakes Ames and covered the next 667 miles. The final 120 miles were built under a contract with J. W. Davis.

These agreements with general contractors were motivated not by a desire to improve the organizational efficiency of construction but by financial considerations. In each case the contractor was merely an agent acting in behalf of the stockholders of the Credit Mobilier. The signing of the agreements with Hoxie, Ames and Davis did not alter the organization of the work or the personnel involved in any material respect from what it would otherwise have been. Durant, Duff, other members of the Union Pacific's board of directors, and the Union Pacific engineers still supervised the work and negotiated with the sub-contractors. What the device of construction contracts accomplished was this: it enabled the stockholders of the Credit Mobilier to come into possession of 367,623 shares of Union Pacific stock as well as large amounts of cash and other securities. The construction contracts provided the legal basis upon which the promoters were able to reap the profit that aroused the ire of the nation.

The Hoxie contract was approved on September 23, 1864. The contractor agreed to build and equip the road for 100 miles. The money for the work of construction was to be supplied by Hoxie, who was to receive Union Pacific bonds as security Hoxie also agreed to purchase $500,000 of Union Pacific stock. In return the contractor was to be paid $50,000 per mile for his work. This amount was made payable either in cash, or in first-mortgage bonds taken at 80 and land-grant bonds taken at 70.

On October 4th, the agreement was extended to cover a total of 247 miles. The Hoxie contract was apparently inspired by Durant to whom the contract was assigned even before it was ratified by the Union Pacific board. Fourteen days after it was ratified, Durant, Bushnell, McComb, Charles A. Lambard and G. G. Gray agreed to provide $1,600,000 for the fulfillment of the Hoxie contract. In order to limit their liability, Durant and his associates had the Hoxie contract transferred to the Credit Mobilier on March 15, 1865, at the same time bringing Sidney Dillon, John Duff and J. M. S. Williams into the venture.[39]

The Ames contract was conditionally agreed to on August 16, 1867. It was ratified by the Union Pacific board of directors on October 1st of the same year. The contract called for the building and equipping of 667 miles at a total cost of $47,915,000. Payment was to be made in cash; but if the railroad could not sell the government bonds at par and the first-mortgage bonds at 90, the difference would be deducted from the payment due to the contractor. In no case could the contractor be charged more than $100 for each bond that sold below $900. If the cash realized on the sale of the government and first-mortgage bonds was not enough to pay the contractor, the contractor agreed to purchase Union Pacific stock in such amounts that the proceeds of the sale would cover the deficiency. On October 15, 1867, Oakes Ames assigned his contract to seven trustees who were to execute the contract and divide the profit among the shareholders of the Credit Mobilier.[40]

The Davis contract was approved on November 1, 1868. Davis agreed to build and equip the remaining portion of the road under " the conditions and terms " of the Ames contract, at a price per mile to be later " established by competent engineers." This contract was assigned to the same trustees that had administered the Ames contract on November 6, 1868. Total payments by the Union Pacific under the Davis contract eventually amounted to over $23,000,000.[41]

[39] Wilson, pp. 63-65, 159-160; Wilson, part II, pp. 2-7; Poland, pp. 60-61.
[40] Wilson, part II, pp. 10-16.
[41] Ibid., pp. 16-17.

The Ames-Durant conflict.

One of the important episodes during the period of construction was the eruption of a struggle for the control of the
Credit Mobilier and the Union Pacific that split the promoters
into two warring factions. Durant had been the dominant
figure in the early stages of the enterprise. It was Durant who
organized the company's first surveys, pushed through the Act
of 1864, secured the Pondir loan and hired the sub-contractors.
Initially he also provided the largest single amount of capital.
About 43 percent of the first $1,400,000 put into the Credit
Mobilier was supplied by Durant; and another 14 percent was
provided by Bushnell, Durant's closest associate.[42] Two of the
individuals that Durant turned to in the course of his search
for additional funds were the brothers Oakes and Oliver Ames.
Oakes Ames was a Congressman with " great influence among
the moneyed men " of Boston. Durant believed that Ames
could " induce a great many persons to go into the Credit
Mobilier " besides being able to invest a sizable amount on
his own account.[43] Events justified Durant's expectations. By
the spring of 1866, Oliver and Oakes Ames had invested

[42] Wilson, p. 160. Durant also appears to have been the person behind the
sudden rush of subscriptions that secured the charter of the Union Pacific. An
article in the *Am. R. R. Jour.*, XXXVII (July 23, 1864), p. 705, stated that
" the whole affair came very near falling into entire ruin by the lapse of the time
to which its organization was limited, when the vigor, capital and influence of a
single person in the city of New York, placed the work on its feet, and from
that moment it walked on its way with renewed vitality. The person arranged
with his associates whom he selected from prominent and influential classes, to
make the necessary subscription in time to save the charter; and had also prepared
himself by minute preliminary examinations and surveys, to give intelligent
opinions not only upon the subject of cost, but of routes and connections." The
article does not identify the individual. However, Durant was the only person
in possession of such detailed surveys in 1863. Wilson, pp. 238-39.

In his testimony before the Poland committee Durant said: " Believing the
enterprise would ultimately succeed, I made my own subscription, and, finding
it impossible to induce capitalists to engage in the enterprise, I succeeded in
obtaining subscriptions for the requisite amount only by inducing my friends to
subscribe, I advancing the money to pay their first installment of ten per cent.
thereon, giving them the option to retain the stock by returning me my advances,
or I would find parties to take the stock off their hands. All of this stock,
amounting to three-fourths of the whole stock ($2,000,000) required to be
subscribed, was subsequently transferred to me, the parties not choosing, even
after the amendment in 1864, to take any risk in the enterprise." Poland, p. 388;
see also Wilson, p. 515.

[43] Wilson, p. 89.

$402,500 and their friends another $400,000. Their group held 32 percent of the stock of the Credit Mobilier, the Durant-Bushnell combination, 27 percent. A year later the stock owned by the Ames group totalled $1,165,700—80 percent more than the amount owned by Durant and Bushnell.[44]

On October 3, 1866, Oliver Ames and his friend, Sidney Dillon, were elected to the board of directors of the Union Pacific. A month later Ames became the president of the company.[45] Control was rapidly passing out of Durant's grasp. Determined to retain some measure of his sovereignty, Durant launched a campaign of harassment against his rivals. In November he signed a contract with a man named L. B. Boomer for the construction of 150 miles of road at prices that barely covered the cost of construction and left little or no room for a profit. The Union Pacific's board of directors ignored the Boomer agreement. On January 5, 1867 it voted to extend the Hoxie contract, which had expired three months earlier. This decision was voided when Durant obtained a court injunction on the ground that the prices charged under the Hoxie agreement were exorbitant![46] In March and in June, Durant again successfully wielded the weapon of injunction to block two more attempted contracts.[47]

By the summer of 1867 it appeared as if the factional battle was stalemated. Oliver Ames had succeeded to the presidency of the railroad and Durant had been ousted from the board of directors of the Credit Mobilier.[48] Yet the onetime ruler of the Union Pacific still retained enough power to frustrate his oppo-

[44] Ibid., pp. 153-56. The Ames group is here taken to include the Ames brothers, Alley, Dillon, Grimes, the members of the Hazard family, Hooper and Williams. Duff seems to have wavered between the two factions. Wilson, pp. 13, 163, 488-89; Poland, pp. 19, 87.

[45] Wilson, pp. 241, 598.

[46] Ibid., pp. 66-69; part II, pp. 7-8.

[47] Wilson, pp. 70-71, 163.

[48] Durant was turned out of the board of directors of the Credit Mobilier on May 18, 1867. Ibid., p. 13.

John Alley, one of the Ames group, said: " Mr. Ames and his friends feeling that it was indispensably necessary (in fact self-preservation required it at the time) that they should get rid of Durant and company [sic]. While not able to turn them out of the direction of the Union Pacific Railroad Company at that time, they had the power to turn Durant and friends out of the Credit Mobilier. They did so, and elected seven directors of the highest character and respectability. . . ." Poland, p. 87.

nents. Durant's maneuvers had not affected the pace of construction. Over 200 miles of line had been completed despite the absence of a contract.[49] The construction contracts were only a legal device for transferring the securities of the Union Pacific to the promoters. Durant had, however, succeeded in delaying the distribution of the company's stocks and bonds. The bottling up of these securities became all the more painful as Bushnell's sales effort began to reveal a change in the marketability of the first-mortgage bonds. Furthermore, the longer the signing of a contract was delayed, the more such a contract would become *ex post facto* so far as actual construction was concerned. Since the promoters had five government directors to contend with, this was a source of considerable embarrassment.

During the period from August through the middle of October a compromise was arranged. Durant agreed to the Oakes Ames contract while the Ames faction agreed to have the contract administered by a group of seven trustees. As long as contracts were assigned to the Credit Mobilier, the affairs of the promoters could be dominated by the Ames party which had enough strength within the construction company to win on any issue. Under the new arrangement each faction had equal power. Three of the trustees—Durant, Bushnell and McComb—were members of the Durant faction; and three—Oliver Ames, Alley and Dillon—belonged to the Ames group. The seventh trustee—Benjamin E. Bates—was apparently a neutral figure.[50] Before the compromise became binding, the Ames faction attempted to dislodge Durant from his last position of power. At the annual meeting of Union Pacific stockholders, held on October 2, 1867, the Ames party put up a ticket for the board of directors which excluded Durant. A bitter battle followed. Each side claimed victory. But the issue was resolved when Durant obtained an injunction against the opposition ticket.[51] Durant had secured his position for at least another year.

[49] Wilson, p. 65; Sabin, *op. cit.*, p. 155; Rhodes, *op. cit.*, p. 5.
[50] Wilson, part II, p. 16.
[51] Poland, pp. 372, 374. In a letter to McComb, Ames wrote: " I do not think we should do right to put Durant in as a director, unless he withdraws his injunction suits and submits to the will of the majority. He cannot hurt us half as badly out of the direction as he can in, and there is no pleasure, peace, safety, or comfort with him unless he agrees to abide the decision of the majority, as the rest of us do." The letter was dated September 17, 1867. Wilson, p. 120.

Compromise was the only practical possibility that remained. On October 15, 1867, the trusteeship agreement was signed.

THE PROFIT

The report of the Wilson committee presented two purportedly complementary estimates of the profit of the promoters. The first, $43,929,328.34, represented the profit calculated at the face value of the securities received by the promoters.[52]

TABLE I

THE WILSON COMMITTEE'S ESTIMATE OF THE PROFIT OF THE PROMOTERS TAKEN AT THE FACE VALUE OF THE SECURITIES OF THE UNION PACIFIC RAILROAD

Cost to the railroad company:		
Hoxie contract...................................		$12,974,416.24
Ames contract...................................		57,140,102.94
Davis contract..................................		23,431,768.10
Total.......................................		93,546,287.28
Cost to the contractors:		
Hoxie contract.....................	$ 7,806,183.33	
Ames contract.....................	27,285,141.99	
Davis contract.....................	15,639,633.62	50,720,958.94
		42,825,328.34
Amount paid to the Credit Mobilier by the Trustees of the Oakes Ames contract on account of fifty-eight miles.........................		1,104,000.00
Total profit on construction.....................		43,929,328.34

Source: Wilson, pp. XIV, 373.

As shown in Table I, it was derived by finding the difference between the payment of the Union Pacific (in cash and securities) to the Credit Mobilier and the trustees of the Ames and Davis contracts and the actual (cash) outlays of the contractors. The second, $23,366,319.81, was put forward as the committee's estimate of the cash value of the first figure. However, this cash profit was not derived directly from the first figure. No attempt was made to separate the $43,929,328.34 into its cash and

[52] This figure is too high. The $1,104,000 payment by the trustees to the Credit Mobilier was a transfer payment. Its inclusion in the profit figure represents double counting. Wilson, pp. 373-75, 641.

security components, thus permitting a determination of the cash value of the latter. The cash profit was determined from a separate source—incomplete abstracts of the books of the Credit Mobilier presented by the company's treasurer. As it turns out, these two estimates are not complementary but contradictory.

Indeed, the cash profit could not have amounted to 23.4 million dollars even if the promoters had drained the railroad of every penny of its uncommitted cash. As shown in Table II, the cash received by the Union Pacific between the time of

TABLE II

ESTIMATE OF THE PROFIT OF THE PROMOTERS ON THE ASSUMPTION THAT THEY
DRAINED ALL OF THE UNCOMMITTED CASH OF THE UNION PACIFIC

Cash Resources:

1.	Cash realized on all bonds.............	$63,463,764.09	
2.	Cash paid on stock..................	351,470.00	
3.	Payment from the Central Pacific.......	2,138,000.00	
4.	Net earnings, 1867-1872..............	13,736,362.90	
5.	Capital of Credit Mobilier.............	3,921,000.00	
6.	Floating debt, January 31, 1873........	2,433,891.25	
7.			$86,044,488.24

Cash Expenditures:

8.	Payments under Hoxie contract........	7,806,183.33	
9.	Payments under Ames and Davis contracts	42,914,774.61	
10.	Expenditures on construction directly by Union Pacific.....................	8,445,313.33	
11.	Interest payments on bonded debt, 1867-1872	13,755,192.22	
12.			72,921,463.49
13.	Maximum cash available for distribution..............		13,123,024.75
14.	Capital of Credit Mobilier.........................		3,921,000.00
15.	Maximum cash available for profit..................		9,202,024.75
16.	Cash value of Union Pacific stock....................		11,028,690.00
17.	Maximum cash profit......................		20,230,714.75

Sources and notes:

LINE 1. Wilson, p. 639. See below, p. 72 for the face value of the various bond issues and the amounts realized on each.

LINE 2. Wilson, pp. 740-43.

LINE 3. PRC, V, p. 3521.

LINE 4. PRC, VIII, pp. 4965, 5266. These are net earnings after the deduction of the one-half charge on government transportation retained by the government.

LINE 5. Wilson, pp. 15, 379-84. The paid-in capital of the Credit Mobilier was $3,750,000. During 1866 and 1867 the stockholders of the Credit Mobilier purchased scrip on 38,000 shares of Union Pacific stock for which they paid $4.50 per share. The total expenditure on these shares, $171,000, has been treated as an addition to capital rather than a deduction from profit. Wilson, pp. 745-48; see also the note to line 9 of Table V, below.

LINE 6. Wilson, p. 595. This amount includes a sterling loan of 120,000 pounds. The value of the pound in 1872 was $4.91 in gold or $5.50 in currency. W. M. Persons, P. M. Tuttle and E. Frickey, " Business and Financial Conditions Following the Civil War in the United States," *The Review of Economic Statistics Supplements*, II (1920), p. 54; James Keith Kindahl, *The Economics of Resumption: The United States 1865-1879* (Unpublished doctoral dissertation, University of Chicago, 1958), p. 13.

LINE 8. Wilson, pp. XIV, 637.

LINE 9. *Ibid.*

LINE 10. *Ibid.*, p. 637.

LINE 11. PRC, VIII, p. 4966; Wilson, p. 637. From the figures given in PRC, $4,902,272.60, the estimated interest on the government bonds, was subtracted.

LINE 16. PRC, VIII, p. 4951. The stock is valued at 30.

its formation in 1863 and December 31, 1872, amounted to $86,044,488.24. The known expenditures on construction and bonded interest during the same period were $72,921,463.49. The difference between the two figures is the maximum amount of cash that could have been distributed to the promoters. Of this amount, only $9,202,024.75 can be considered profit, since $3,921,000.00 represents the capital of the Credit Mobilier. Adding the estimated value of the entire issue of Union Pacific stock, we arrive at $20,230,714.75 as the greatest possible cash value of the profit of the promoters. However, this figure is too high to be useful even as an upper limit. It is based on the assumption that the corporation could have functioned without a cent of working capital. Moreover, while Table II is comprehensive with respect to receipts, it is not comprehensive with respect to expenditures. Certain charges, such as the interest on the floating debt, are omitted.[53] Yet even this exaggerated maximum profit is a full three million dollars less than the figure projected by the Wilson committee.

It is considerably easier to demonstrate the implausibility of the Wilson estimate than to replace it with the correct one. There are as many estimates of the profit of the promoters as

[53] *Ibid.*, pp. 200, 212.

there are studies of the subject. Rowland Hazard suggested that the true amount was $15,000,000 while J. B. Crawford put the figure at $8,141,903.70. Henry Kirk White's study led him to conclude that the promoters realized $16,710,432.82. John P. Davis, using several methods of estimation, arrived at figures that differed from each other by as much as $17,000,000. More recently, George A. Donely, using a technique somewhat more sophisticated than those of his predecessors, placed the profit at $13,712,368.[54] The great dispersion in these estimates is due partly to the contradictions in the Wilson report and partly to certain inherent limitation in the material on which such valuations must be based. The bookkeeping systems of the Union Pacific and the Credit Mobilier were " disgraceful "; the financial records contained in the report and hearings of the Wilson committee are fragmentary; the market value of the securities in which the promoters were paid is uncertain. Indeed, these factors make a precise determination of the profit of the promoters impossible. Fortunately, for the purposes of this study, a precise determination of the profit of the promoters is not necessary. It is sufficient to know the range within which the actual profit must have fallen or, more specifically, the upper limit of that range.

Since the entire profit of the promoters came out of the payments made by the Union Pacific to the contractors,[55] the starting figure in the calculation of an upper limit is $93,546,287.28. Of this amount, approximately $36,752,300.00 was paid for in Union Pacific stock. The balance, $56,783,987.28, represents the maximum amount of cash that could have been paid by the railroad to the contractors. Out of this balance, $50,720,958.94 was paid in cash for the work performed under the Hoxie, Ames and Davis contracts, leaving $6,063,028.34. An additional

[54] Roland Hazard, *The Credit Mobilier of America* (Providence: Sidney S. Rider, 1881), pp. 27-29; Crawford, *op. cit.*, pp. 71-72; Henry Kirk White, *History of the Union Pacific Railway* (Chicago: University of Chicago Press, 1895), pp. 35-37; John P. Davis, *Union Pacific Railway, op. cit.*, pp. 170-73; George Anthoney Donely, *The Construction of the Union Pacific Railway by the Credit Mobilier of America* (Unpublished Master's essay, Columbia University, 1958), pp. 78-79.

[55] The Credit Mobilier was the contractor for the Hoxie contract and the seven trustees were the contractors of the Ames and Davis contracts. However, as indicated above (pp. 61-62, 65), the trustees were merely agents of the stockholders of the Credit Mobilier.

$589,958.12 must be deducted since the contractors were charged the difference between 90 and the actual price at which the first-mortgage bonds were sold. The remainder, $5,473,070.22, represents the maximum amount of cash that could have been distributed among the promoters as profit. Adding the cash value of the stock, we find that the upper limit on the range of possible profits is $16,501,760.22. (See Table III.)

TABLE III

ESTIMATE OF THE UPPER LIMIT OF THE PROFIT OF THE PROMOTERS

1.	Payment to contractors at face value of securities..........	$93,546,287.28
2.	Less stock at face value.............................	36,762,300.00
3.	Maximum amount of cash paid to contractors............	56,783,987.28
4.	Less cash payments to sub-contractors..................	50,720,958.94
5.		6,063,028.34
6.	Less discount on first-mortgage bonds charged to contractors	589,958.12
7.	Maximum amount of cash available for distribution as profit	5,473,070.22
8.	Plus value of Union Pacific stock taken at 30............	11,028,690.00
9	Estimated upper limit on profit................	16,501,760.22

Sources and notes:

LINE 1. Wilson, p. XIV.

LINE 2. PRC, VIII, p. 4951; Wilson, pp. 20-21, 163-64, 740-50. Approximately 23,670 shares of Union Pacific stock were purchased by cash subscribers. Thus only 343,953 shares were actually issued as payment on the construction contracts. However, the Credit Mobilier purchased virtually all of the holdings of the original subscribers. The purchase of these 23,670 shares (apparently at face value, i. e., at the price paid by the cash subscribers) reduced the cash value of the capital of the Credit Mobilier. In calculating the profit of the promoters this capital loss has to be deduced. The result is exactly the same if all of the stock is treated as payment on the contracts and the Credit Mobilier is presumed not to have suffered a capital loss. The latter procedure is followed because it simplifies the exposition.

LINE 4. Wilson, pp. XIV, 637.

LINE 6. The Ames and Davis contracts charged the promoters for any discount on the first-mortgage bonds below 90. The amount of bonds issued under these contracts amounted to approximately $20,750,559 at face value. The average price at which the bonds actually sold was 87.156905. Wilson, pp. 65, 639; Wilson, part II, pp. 11-12, 17; PRC, VIII, p. 4951.

LINE 8. PRC, VIII, p. 4951.

The last figure will exceed the actual profit of the promoters if they incurred expenses not taken into account in Table III. However, such expenses, if they existed, could not have been very great. The promoters are known to have distributed cash assets (cash plus first-mortgage bonds taken at their average market value of 87.16) amounting to at least $9,475,000. The cash fund out of which this distribution could have been made appears to have totalled $11,852,000—of which $5,473,000 was profit, $3,921,000 was capital, $1,125,000 was cash realized on the sale of 28,125 shares of Union Pacific stock, and $1,333,000 was cash realized on bond transactions in 1869-70.[56] Unless there were additional sales of stock not revealed by the record, the omitted expenses, if any, must have been less than $2,400,000. Account should also be taken of the possibility that 30 might have been too high a figure at which to value the stock of the Union Pacific. Approximately 54,000 shares of this stock were received by the promoters when the average price appears to have been about 10.[57] Making the necessary allowances for omitted expenses and a possible overvaluation of the stock, the lower limit of the profit of the promoters appears to have been about $13,000,000.

The Wilson committee fell into another error when it contended that the total cost of constructing the Union Pacific was $50,720,959—the sum of the expenditures by the contractors under the Hoxie, Ames and Davis contracts. This figure neglected $8,445,313 spent directly by the Union Pacific on such items as engineering fees; the construction of stations, shops, bridges and fences; the purchase of equipment; and interest on construction loans.[58] Hence the actual cost of building the railroad from Omaha to Promontory Point was $59,166,272.

---

[56] Wilson, pp. XV-XVI, 630; above, Table III, line 7. The details of the 1869-70 bond transactions are given in Appendix A.

[57] *Ibid.*, pp. 166, 657, 740-49.

[58] *Ibid.*, pp. XVII, 637. The following are the main items that comprised the 8.4 million dollar figure:

Discount and interest (on short-term loans)....	$2,581,180
Equipment	1,460,676
Engineering	890,866
Station buildings........................	730,388
Preliminary expenses.....................	487,230
Expense	421,968
Shops and tools..........................	398,429
Snow-sheds	293,570
Fencing	249,428
Legal expense...........................	235,009

However, the section of the road lying between Promontory Point and Ogden was sold to the Central Pacific in 1869 for $2,138,000.[59] Since the cost of constructing the line held by the Union Pacific at the time of the Wilson hearing was $57,028,272, the committee's assertion that the proceeds of the sales of the government and first-mortgage bonds covered the cost of construction was also incorrect. Construction charges consumed not only the entire proceeds of the government and first-mortgage bonds but also the entire proceeds of the land-grant bonds.

TABLE IV

BONDED DEBT OF THE UNION PACIFIC

	Face value	Proceeds from sales	Face value of bonds outstanding in 1872
Government bonds	$27,236,512	$27,145,163	$27,236,512
First-mortgage bonds	27,213,00	23,718,009	27,213,000
Land-grant bonds	10,400,000	6,063,992	9,068,500 [1]
Income bonds	9,335,000	6,536,600	9,335,000

[1] This figure was derived by averaging the amount of bonds outstanding on December 31, 1871, with those outstanding on December 31, 1872.

Sources: Wilson, p. 639; PRC, VIII, pp. 5059, 5061.

As in the case of the profit, the inadequacy of the records makes impossible a precise determination of the amount of capital put up by the promoters and the time span over which it was invested. As shown in Table V, the available data seem to indicate an investment span of about six years. The accumulated average amount of the investment appears to have been $340,000 in 1864, $1,750,000 in 1865, $2,750,000 in 1866, $3,530,000 in 1867, and $3,920,000 in the years 1868 and 1869. The average investment for the entire six year period was about $2,700,000. If the same amount of capital had been invested in long-term government bonds, which then yielded 6.02 percent,[60] the promoters would have earned $1,086,000—less than

[59] PRC, V, p. 3521. The amount realized by the Union Pacific is put at $2,698,620 in Wilson, p. 637. The difference between these two figures is negligible; it has no significant effect on any of the questions discussed below.

[60] The average price on the government bonds issued to the company was 99.664608. They paid six percent in currency on the face value. Wilson, p. 639.

one-eleventh of the profit they reaped from the construction of
the Union Pacific.

TABLE V

ESTIMATE OF THE CAPITAL INVESTED BY PROMOTERS
(In thousands of dollars)

	Year	Month	Approximate accumulated amount of investment	Accumulated average investment in given year
1.	1864	Jan.-Sept.	218	344
2.		Oct.	667	
3.		Nov.-Dec.	751	
4.	1865	Jan.-March	751	1,751
5.		April-July	1,751	
6.		Aug.-Dec.	2,351	
7.	1866	Jan.-March	2,351	2,755
8.		April-Oct.	2,851	
9.		Nov.-Dec.	3,022	
10.	1867	Jan.-March	3,022	3,531
11.		April-May	3,617	
12.		June	3,633	
13.		July-Nov.	3,703	
14.		Dec.	3,921	
15.	1868	Jan.-Dec.	3,921	3,921
16.	1869	Jan.-Dec.	3,921	3,921
17.	Average investment for the entire period............			2,704

Sources and notes:

LINE 1. Initial payment on Union Pacific stock. Wilson, pp. 740-42; Poland,
p. 388.

LINE 2. Additional payments on Union Pacific stock plus a one-fourth payment
by the assignees of the Hoxie contract on their pledged amount. Wilson, p. 742;
Wilson, part II, pp. 4-5.

LINE 3. Additional payments on Union Pacific stock. Wilson, pp. 742-43.

LINE 5. Additional capital paid in at time of the activization of the Credit
Mobilier. Wilson, p. 160.

LINE 6. Capital stock of the Credit Mobilier raised to $2,000,000. Wilson,
p. 160; Poland, p. 19.

LINE 8. Capital stock of Credit Mobilier raised to $2,500,000. Wilson, p. 154.

LINE 9. The Credit Mobilier sold $3,800,000 of scrip on Union Pacific stock
to its stockholders at 4.5 cents on the dollar. Over 95 percent of these sales took
place between August and December, 1866. The balance was sold in early 1867.
The full amount has been arbitrarily assigned to November, 1866. Wilson, pp.

TABLE V (Continued)

382, 384, 745-48. In testifying before the Wilson committee Ham put the face value of the scrip purchased at $5,000,000. However, the table in Wilson, pp. 745-48, shows this figure to be too high.

LINE 11. Sale, during March and April, of Credit Mobilier stock issue authorized in February, 1867. Wilson, pp. 15, 619.

LINE 12. Increased by the sale of Credit Mobilier stock during May and June. Wilson, pp. 19, 619. Reduced by the amount of cash paid in on subscriptions for Union Pacific stock. Ham and Williams testified that virtually all of the stock held by original cash subscribers was purchased by the Credit Mobilier. The dates of the purchases are uncertain. The full amount has been arbitrarily assigned to this month on the assumption that the Credit Mobilier was too short of funds to have purchased large amounts at an earlier date. Wilson, pp. 20-21, 163-64.

LINE 13. Sale of Credit Mobilier stock during July. Wilson, p. 19.

LINE 14. Sale of Credit Mobilier stock. Wilson, p. 19.

LINE 16. As of December 31, 1868, the Union Pacific had issued only $20,762,000 in stock. Another 80,000 shares were issued at various times during 1869. Between October and the end of the year, the promoters retrieved about 30 percent of their capital. Most of the rest was recovered during the first six months of 1870. The assumption that the entire capital was retrieved on December 31, 1869, yields approximately the same result as a calculation based on the gradual reduction of the capital over a period of a year and a half. Wilson, pp. 749-50; PRC, VIII, pp. 5041, 5053, 5079.

THE NATURE AND EXTENT OF THE RISK FACED BY THE PROMOTERS

If the men who built the Union Pacific " assumed great risks from which others shrank," said the authors of the Wilson report, " they should have all due credit. But we think they differed from other capitalists, not in taking a risk, but in having discovered that the road could be built at vast profit without risk. . . ." [61] Unfortunately time has tended to harden this dictum of the Wilson committee into a historical fact, thus choking off further investigation of the nature and extent of the risk that confronted the promoters. Yet this matter of risk is the crucial issue on which every analysis of the construction of the first Pacific road must hang. No moral judgement on the profit of the promoters can be made, no responsibility for the financial emasculation of the road assigned, no decision concerning the efficacy of the Acts of 1862 and 1864 rendered, without first thoroughly probing this issue.

[61] *Ibid.*, p. XX.

The argument behind the Wilson position can be framed in the following manner: Certainly there were risks connected with the building of a Pacific road. There had been great doubt as to whether a road built hundreds of miles across a wasteland could earn enough to provide the market rate of return on the capital invested in it. However, these risks were irrelevant so far as the promoters were concerned. The promoters did not look to the future earnings of the road for their profit. They sought their return in the spread between the cost of construction and the value of the bonds issued by the government and the railroad. Since the value of these securities exceeded the cost of construction by a considerable margin, the building of the Union Pacific was a riskless enterprise for the men of the Credit Mobilier.

This argument is, of course, entirely fallacious. The fact that the promoters looked to construction rather than the future earnings of the road did not eliminate the element of risk—it merely changed the nature of the risk. Since the promoters were paid either in the securities of the Union Pacific or out of the proceeds of the sale of these securities, the size of their profit depended on the prices of the bonds and the stock. The promoters reaped a profit of, say, 16.5 million dollars because they realized 87 on the first-mortgage bonds and 30 on the stock. If, however, the market had been such that the promoters were unable to sell the bonds for more than 60, their profit would have been reduced by 7.4 million dollars. If the first-mortgage bonds had sold for 40, their profits would have been reduced by 12.8 million dollars. Similarly, if the stock of the Union Pacific had sold for 20 instead of 30, their profit would have been reduced by 3.7 million dollars. Had the stock sold at 20 and the bonds at 60, the profit of the promoters would have been 5.5 million dollars and the average annual rate of return on their investment would have been about 30 percent. Taking the bonds at 40 and the stock at 10, there would have been, not a profit, but a loss of 3.6 million dollars—almost the entire capital invested by the promoters.

These calculations are not irrelevant theorizing. Quite the contrary. The record suggests that the market for the securities of the Union Pacific was extremely weak prior to the middle of 1867. John Alley testified that the first-mortgage bonds were

" entirely unsalable [in early 1867] at 40 and 50 cents on the
dollar, and in some instances at 25 cents on the dollar." There
were " very few capitalists," he continued, " who had faith
enough in the successful prosecution of the undertaking to feel
it was safe to invest a dollar in the bonds, or even to take the
notes of the company, with the bonds as collateral, at 60 cents
on the dollar without a large commission." [62] Benjamin Ham,
the treasurer of the Credit Mobilier, made a similar statement.[63]
And Cornelius Bushnell testified that as late as the spring of
1867, " Mr. Duff thought it would be impossible to sell the
Union Pacific Railroad bonds until they extended the line to
some place where the cars would be running, and I contended
that the affair would be an utter failure if we had to wait
until that time." [64] The market situation of the Union Pacific's
stock was even weaker than that of the bonds. John Duff
asserted that Union Pacific stock could not be sold " except to
people who would take a risk as they would at a faro-bank." [65]
J. M. S. Williams argued that the stock was not worth ten
cents on the dollar.[66] These contentions were supported by
government director Charles T. Sherman.[67]

That the investing public had grave reservations concerning
the profitability of a Pacific road is beyond dispute. " The
enterprise," said Henry V. Poor, " was indeed hazardous in
the extreme." " Vast wastes " had to be traversed. " Three
lofty mountain ranges," far " more formidable " than those
encountered by any previous road, had to be crossed. The
materials for the super-structure had to be imported " from
Eastern States, or from England." The men " who undertook
the construction of the Pacific Railroad," Poor concluded, " were
leaders of a forlorn hope. To be connected with it was enough
not only to imperil one's money, but to forfeit one's reputation
for business sagacity." [68] Horace Clark, son-in-law of Cornelius
Vanderbilt and one of the leading railroad men of the time,
refused to join in the promotion of the road despite the possi-

[62] *Ibid.*, pp. 557-58; cf. PRC, V, pp. 3493-94.
[63] Poland, p. 148.
[64] Wilson, p. 41.
[65] *Ibid.*, p. 492.
[66] *Ibid.*, p. 166.
[67] *Ibid.*, p. 657.
[68] Poor, *loc. cit.*, pp. 667, 677.

bility of reaping "a very large profit." "I did not invest a dollar in it," he said, because "I thought the money invested would be a total loss." In his judgement "the hazard to the contractors was . . . not that they could not build the road; but that, when the road was built, it would be worth nothing." [69] Since the prices of the securities of the Union Pacific depended on the public's expectations of the future earnings of the road, the extreme doubt attached to the earning capacity of the road in the early years of construction necessarily implied a low price on the company's bonds and an even lower price on its stock.

The behaviour pattern of the promoters also suggests a low price for the securities of the Union Pacific. Had there been a reasonable market for the first-mortgage bonds in 1865, Durant's problem of raising money for construction would have been solved. He need not have borrowed at rates of interest as high as 19 percent per year.[70] More important, he need not have diluted, and eventually sacrificed, his control for the million dollars brought into the venture by the Ames group. A low price on the first-mortgage bonds is implied by the reluctance shown by investors toward the purchase of Credit Mobilier stock in the spring of 1867 even when they were given first-mortgage bonds equal, at face value, to their investment. If the bonds were near the price of 90 or 95 that they reached some nine months later, investors would have been purchasing $1,250,000 of Credit Mobilier stock at effective prices ranging from zero to ten dollars per share (since the stock sold at money prices ranging from 95 to par).[71] It is hard to explain the difficulty the promoters had in placing this stock if these were, in fact, the effective prices at which the issue was being offered.

Finally, deductive analysis provides some support for the prices of the securities cited by Alley and the others. From the records we have the following information: (1) Through the early period the promoters were borrowing money at rates of interest between one and one and one-half percent per month.[72] (2) A large number of first-mortgage bonds were sold at about

[69] Wilson, p. 434.

[70] *Ibid.*, p. 252; above, p. 59. One and one-half percent per month compounded is 19.6 percent per year.

[71] Wilson, p. 41.

[72] Above, p. 59.

80.[73] (3) In the fall of 1865 the promoters made the then sanguine forecast that they would have 200 miles of line completed by August, 1867.[74] (4) Even after 305 miles of line were completed (December, 1866), most of the promoters still felt that the market for bonds was too weak to permit a public sales campaign.[75] Given the fact that in 1865, 1866 and 1867 the promoters preferred to borrow at rates as high as one and one-half percent per month rather than market their bonds, and given the fact that after the middle of 1867 they marketed a considerable proportion of the bonds at 80, we could, if we knew the date at which they expected the bonds to reach 80, deduce the maximum first-mortgage bond market prices that could have prevailed prior to the summer of 1867. From the information cited above, it seems reasonable to infer that prior to the summer of 1867, the promoters expected to have to wait until early 1869 before the bonds reached a price of 80.[76] This implies that the most the bonds could have sold for was 63 in early 1866 and 69 in early 1867. Although these figures are higher than those cited by Alley, they are well below the price put on them by the Wilson committee in its calculations. Moreover, the deduced figures are maximum prices. The actual prices could well have been and very likely were, as Alley claimed, below 40 or even below 25.

Thus the promoters were not in quite as fortunate a position as the Congressional investigators believed. The men involved in the Union Pacific " ring " had not discovered a magic formula for profit without risk. The risk they faced was twofold: First, the promoters gambled on the possibility that the prices of the Union Pacific's securities would become high enough to provide them with the funds needed to complete the work of construction before the exhaustion of their own financial resources forced the abandonment of the project. Secondly, they gambled that the prices of the securities would eventually become high

[73] Wilson, pp. 23, 35, 78.

[74] U. S. Congress, House, *Report of the Secretary of Interior, 1865*, 39th Cong., 1st Sess., Exec. Docs. No. 1 (1248), pp. xii-xiii.

[75] Wilson, pp. 40-41, 492, 558.

[76] When Duff spoke of delaying the bond sale until "they extended the line to some place where the cars would be running," (see above, p. 76) he apparently had the Mormon community in Utah, the first sizable settlement west of Nebraska, in mind. This settlement was not reached until the spring of 1869.

enough to allow them to recoup their investment and realize a
profit. Even if the promoters did not look to the future earnings
of the road as the fund from which they expected to obtain
their profit, their financial fate depended on these earnings, or
more precisely, on the public's expectations with respect to
these earnings. The unique feature of the Credit Mobilier was
not that it eliminated or even reduced the element of risk, but
that it provided the promoters with the possibility of obtaining
a profit large enough to induce them to undertake the venture
despite the risk.

One important question has, until now, been by-passed. What
was responsible for the sharp reversal in the attitude of the
investing public toward the Union Pacific Railroad that apparently took place between the spring and winter of 1867? The
main factor in this change seems to have been the deep impression made on the press and the public by the spectacular and
entirely unexpected, speed with which construction was pushed.

In his report for 1865, the Secretary of the Interior euphe-
mistically said that the " energy displayed " in the prosecution
of the construction of the Union Pacific " for two or three years
did not . . . equal public expectations and the wishes of the
Government." [77] Sabin points out that " through several years
of actual construction work the Pacific Railway lacked adver-
tising other than that put out by its companies in prospectuses
and reports and the financial departments of the public prints." [78]
In the few articles that did appear in the regular press, much
was unfavorable. For example, in late 1864 a writer for the
Atlantic Monthly lamented that " the great highway of the
continent has been left, *pendente lite*, in the hands of squabbling
speculators and . . . personal recriminations bar the progress of
our commerce between sea and sea." [79]

The burst of speed shown in construction during 1866 found
almost immediate reaction in the press. Between mid-March
and mid-September, 180 miles of track were laid.[80] In August of
1866 the *Commercial and Financial Chronicle* published its first

[77] *Op. cit.*, p. xii.
[78] Sabin, *op. cit.*, p. 109.
[79] Ludlow, *loc. cit.*, p. 605.
[80] Sabin, *op. cit.*, p. 146.

laudatory comment on the rate of construction.[81] In September the same paper " heartily " congratulated the " active minds and hands that have so industriously forwarded the works " and expressed its confidence " that in a few years we shall have the iron rails crossing the Continent over at least one line." [82] The " construction year of 1866 closed upon December 11 with the astounding record of 260 miles of track laid in exactly eight months," said Sabin. " No such railroad building ever had been dreamed of." [83]

The continuation of this rate of construction in 1867 had a snowballing effect on public opinion. The *Chicago Tribune* printed " a daily progress report on the amount of track laid." [84] By mid-1867 the " world's record in track construction had been broken by the march of two and one-half miles in one day and 150 miles in 100 consecutive days. The East was awakening to the significance of the hail in the corridors of her hotels as the omnibuses clattered up: ' Passengers for the Pacific Railroad! ' Interested travellers began to flock by Northwestern railroad and by ferry and 'bus into ' Train Town,' the Union Pacific suburb of Omaha, to view the miracle being achieved beyond where the sun sank in a Brierstadt canvas. The eager newspaper correspondent was out there, his pencil poised, his eyes roving, his ears thirsty." [85] The entry of the road into Cheyenne in October of 1867 was a national event. The *New York Tribune* greeted it with the words, " five hundred miles of civilization." [86]

By the winter of 1867 it was clear that no physical obstacle would prevent the completion of the road. Evans pass, the easy route across the eastern Rocky Mountains, was known. The Central Pacific had completed construction across the Sierra Nevada Mountains. Before it now lay hundreds of miles of flat terrain that assured easy and rapid construction.[87]

The promoters of the Union Pacific have often been condemned for the " excessive " speed with which they pushed the

[81] *Commercial and Financial Chronicle*, III (August 25, 1866), p. 248.
[82] *Ibid.*, (September 8, 1866), p. 311.
[83] Sabin, *op. cit.*, pp. 146-47.
[84] Carl Raymond Gray, *The Significance of the Pacific Railroads*, The Cyrus Fogg Brackett Lectureship (Princeton University, April 9, 1935), p. 15.
[85] Sabin, *op. cit.*, p. 156.
[86] Rhodes, VII, *op. cit.*, p. 5.
[87] Sabin, *op. cit.*, pp. 160-61.

construction of the road. This speed, which added millions of dollars to the expenditure on construction, was motivated by the desire of the promoters to acquire the lion's share of the government largess—a share that might otherwise have fallen to the Central Pacific. But speed of construction was a two-edged sword. Its impact on public opinion, more than any other thing, accounted for the change in the marketability of the Union Pacific's bonds. If speed increased the expenditure on construction, it also saved the road from collapse for want of funds.[88]

To know that the promoters incurred great risk is not enough. Analysis of the causes of the financial enervation of the Union Pacific requires the quantification of the degree of risk. Such quantification is unavoidable. It is explicit or implicit in every study that has been made of the construction and financing of the Union Pacific. The Wilson committee put the probability that the promoters would lose their investment at zero. Hence they implied that the promoters were entitled to a return no greater than the return that they would have earned by investing in the highest grade of securities plus, perhaps, an additional sum for the wages of management. Similarly, those who, like Crawford and Hazard, justified the profit of the promoters, must have arrived at some estimate of the probability of a loss, although they never specified a figure. Quantification of the degree of the risk is the essential prerequisite for the establishment of a "reasonable" profit.

The market prices of the Union Pacific's securities provide a basis for the desired quantification.[89] Alley's statement that first-

[88] The promoters claimed that the speed of construction increased expenditures by about 25 percent. This increased expenditure does not necessarily imply that the *cost* of the road was greater under the condition of rapid construction than it would have been under the condition of slow construction. The question is discussed below, in note 21, p. 104.

[89] Unfortunately there are no published quotations on the prices of Union Pacific securities during the critical years from 1864 to mid-1867, despite the many attempts made by the promoters to market the company's first-mortgage bonds. Prior to the Bushnell campaign, sales were sought through extensive private canvassing rather than advertised offerings. The first quotation on Union Pacific bonds appeared in the comprehensive railroad bond list of the *Commercial and Financial Chronicle* on September 5, 1868. The first quotation on the stock appeared on March 26, 1870. Hence it is necessary to rely on the testimony presented before the Wilson committee for the prices of these securities during the period prior to mid-1867.

mortgage bonds were unmarketable at 40 implied that investors
would not have purchased the bonds unless they had been
offered a rate of return greater than 21.3 percent over a period
of the life of the bonds.[90] Government bonds of the same
maturity yielded 6.02 percent.[91] The differential in the rate of
return on these two securities reflected the market's evaluation
of the risk that the Union Pacific would fail. This risk can be
quantified by interpreting the decision problem that confronted
potential purchasers of the first-mortgage bonds in terms of a
two-point probability distribution. If the road succeeded (i. e.,
if the road was able to meet its contractual obligations to the
bond holders), investors would have received a rate of return
of 21.3 percent on their money; if the road failed, the rate of
return would have been much lower. Assuming that investors
expected to receive a zero rate of return over the life of the
bonds (30 years) if the road failed; assuming also that investors
purchased bonds until the expected rate of return on a security
was equal to the rate of return on government bonds,[92] the
following equation can be established:

(1) $$Op + 21.3(1 - p) = 6.02$$

where p is the market's estimate of the probability that the road
would fail. Solving the equation we find that p equals .717.
In other words, if the assumptions made in equation (1) are
valid, the market price of the first-mortgage bonds implies that
investors believed the probability that the road would fail (i. e.,
that the road would not be completed, or that if completed, the
road would be unable to pay the interest on its bonds) to be
approximately 72 percent.

The usefulness of this estimate depends on the nature of the
assumptions that underly it. In this connection it is important
to note that the assumptions are such that they lead to an under-
statement of the market's evaluation of the probability that the

[90] These were six percent, 30 year bonds with the principal and interest payable
in gold. Gold was 1.414 in 1867. *Commercial and Financial Chronicle*, VI,
(April 25, 1868), p. 525; James Keith Kindahl, *The Economics of Resumption:
The United States 1865-1879* (Unpublished doctoral dissertation, University of
Chicago, 1958), p. 13.
[91] See note 60, p. 72, above.
[92] These assumptions are discussed below.

road would fail. The estimate of p is biased downward in two respects. (1) The equation implies that investors were willing to purchase first-mortgage bonds at 40 although Alley testified that they could not be sold at that price. (2) The assumption that investors would have received a zero rate of return on their investment over the 30 year period if the road failed is quite extreme. It implies that investors believed that the road would fail after the first interest payment and that they would lose all of their original investment in the ensuing reorganization. The assumption of a higher rate of return in the case of default (more generally, the assumption of any distribution of rates of return in the case of default with a mean greater than zero) would have increased the value of p.[93] Consequently, the market price of the bonds implies that investors thought that the probability that the road would fail was *at least* .717.

Equating the expected value of the probability distribution to the rate of return on riskless securities implies that the marginal utility of income of investors was constant. The usual assumption is that the marginal utility of income of investors is declining. This would seem to suggest that our estimate contains an upward as well as a downward bias. However, while the estimate of p would be biased upward *if every person in the market* had had a declining marginal utility of income, as long as the marginal utility of income of some investors (with enough capital to absorb the issue) had been increasing, the assumption of a constant marginal utility intensifies the downward bias.

The assumption of a constant marginal utility of income is justifiable on the ground that the Union Pacific's first-mortgage bonds could have been purchased in units that cost only $400 each. Thus the purchase of a single bond would have involved

---

[93] The mathematical proof of this statement is as follows:

Let p_i be the probability that if the road failed the investors would receive a rate of return of x_i percent on their investment.

Then $p = \sum p_i$ is the probability that the road will fail.

And $\sum x_i p_i$ is the expected rate of return if the road failed.

And $(1 - p) = (1 - \sum p_i)$ is the probability that the road will succeed.

Then, $\sum x_i p_i + 21.3(1 - \sum p_i) = 6.02$ or

$$\sum p_i = \frac{15.28 + \sum x_i p_i}{21.3}$$

Hence if the $\sum x_i p_i \geqq 0$, the $\sum p_i$ will be a minimum when $\sum x_i p_i = 0$.

cnly a very small segment of the utility function of a prosperous investor. Over such a small segment of the utility function, the marginal utility of income would have been approximately constant. In less esoteric language, the equation implies that if the gamble had been "fair," many investors would have been willing to risk a small amount of their wealth (i. e., willing to buy a few bonds each) against the prospect of a very large return and/or a few investors would have been willing to risk a large amount of their wealth; and that these two groups would have possessed enough capital to absorb the entire issue.[94]

With information on the market's evaluation of the probability that the Union Pacific would fail, it is possible to estimate the amount of profit to which the men of the Credit Mobilier were "entitled"—that is, the amount of profit that had to be offered in order to induce investors to undertake the construction of the Union Pacific. The investment decision confronting the promoters may also be analysed in terms of a two-point probability distribution. These men gambled their capital against the possibility of earning a very large profit. The arrangement would have been "fair" if the expected value of the gamble was equal to the amount the promoters could have earned by investing in riskless securities (government bonds). Through June, 1867—the period of great risk—the promoters invested 3.633 million dolars. Assuming that the promoters expected the outcome of the gamble to have been determined by January 1, 1868,[95] we have:

$$(2) \qquad\qquad -3.663p + x(1-p) = .531$$

where x is the profit that was needed to induce the promoters to undertake the construction of the road. Since the promoters would have lost their entire investment if the road failed, we may substitute .717 for p. The value of x that satisfies this equation is 11.1 million dollars. Thus the risk faced by the promoters seems to have "justified" a profit considerably greater than the one the Congressional investigators apparently

[94] Since the Union Pacific operated in a competitive capital market, the assumption of a constant marginal utility of income implies that the supply schedule of funds facing the firm was perfectly elastic at an expected rate of return (in the mathematical sense) equal to the market rate of return.

[95] The significance of this assumption is discussed in note 96, p. 85, below.

had in mind. Deduction based on the market price of the first-mortgage bonds suggests that 11.1 million dollars was a " reasonable " profit.[96]

This analysis of risk need not be interpreted as a vindication of the promoters. The profit they appear to have reaped is still two to five million dollars greater than the " reasonable " amount. The men who built the Union Pacific attributed their bonanza to a lucky accident—the finding of Evans pass, an easy route through the Rocky Mountains—that saved " four, five or six million dollars " on the Ames contract.[97] At first, " I thought I should make about 20 per cent. profit," said Oakes

---

[96] The size of the " justifiable " profit depends on the date on which the promoters expected the outcome of the gamble to be determined. If it is assumed that the promoters had a decision horizon six months greater than the one specified in the text, the " justifiable " profit would be increased by three percent. If, on the other hand, they had expected the gamble to have been determined on July 1, 1867, the " justifiable " profit would be reduced by six percent. As indicated on p. 78, above, the available evidence suggests the longer rather than the shorter time period. Hence 11.1 million dollars is a conservative estimate of the " justifiable " profit. If the shortest possible time horizon were chosen, the " justifiable " profit would become 10.3 million dollars. The difference between this figure and the one given in the text is negligible; it has no significant effect on any of the questions discussed below.

It is possible to estimate the " justifiable " profit by another method. The starting point of this alternate method is also the market price of the first-mortgage bonds.

The statement that the first-mortgage bonds could not have been sold at 40 implies that prospective purchasers were offered at least $212.10 a year for 30 years plus $2,500 at the end of the period, if the road succeeded, for every $1,000 they invested. The *conditional* present value of these payments (i. e., the present value of the payments, if the road succeeded) was $3,346. Hence investors refused to purchase securities that had a conditional present value of 3.346 times the amount of the investment.

Since the promoters were, in effect, investing in the securities of the road, the market price of the bonds suggests that in order to induce the promoters to undertake the construction of the Union Pacific they had to be offered securities with a conditional present value of at least $3.346 for every dollar they invested. Through June, 1867, the promoters invested $3,633,000. Consequently, if they had received the securities of the road at the moment they made their investment, they would have been " entitled " to securities with a conditional present value of $12,156,000. However, the promoters received their securities on an average of over two years after they made their investments. Taking this into account, the promoters were " entitled " to securities with a conditional present value, *at the time they received the securities*, of $14,139,000. Subtracting the amount of their investment, the " justifiable " profit is $10,506,000.

Cf. with the discussion of conditional cost on p. 105, below.

[97] Poland, p. 180.

Ames. It was only " after this contract was made and after we found the easy grade over the Rocky Mountains, [that] I thought we would make a great deal of money." [98] This statement was untrue. The promoters not only knew about Evans pass but formally adopted it as the route of the Union Pacific at a meeting of the railroad's board of directors held on January 5, 1867—seven months before the initial agreement on the Ames contract and nine months before the ratification of the document.[99] Since the Ames contract was signed with full knowledge of the easy route, the greater the expected saving, the more deliberate were the promoters in the inflation of their profit. Thus historians who are inclined to stress the moral turbidity of the promoters need not change their characterizations simply because the promoters faced great risk. On the other hand, those inclined to a softer view can, if they so desire, follow the argument of Charles Francis Adams, Jr. "The country," said this railroad reformer, " has . . . little right to complain if the daring and energetic men, who risked their whole fortunes in the work of forcing through a novel enterprise to a splendid success, now claim to the uttermost farthing the great stakes for which they played so well." [100]

THE FUNDAMENTAL DEFICIENCY IN THE ACTS OF 1862 AND 1864

Clearly, the charge that profiteering was the root cause of the financial enervation of the Union Pacific was based on a compound of errors that included the overestimation of the profit of the promoters, the underestimation of the cost of construction, and the omission of the element of risk. The railroad would have tottered on the brink of bankruptcy even if the promoters had scrupulously limited their profit to the amount " justified " by the risk they had borne. The reduction of the profit of the promoters from 16.5 million dollars to 11.1 million dollars would have left the Union Pacific with 5.4 million dollars in cash. With this sum the road could have liquidated its

[98] Wilson, p. 28.

[99] The documentation on this point is given in Appendix B.

[100] Charles Francis Adams, Jr., " Railway Problems in 1869," *North American Review*, CX (1870), pp. 117-18.

TABLE VI

UNION PACIFIC EARNINGS AND INTEREST ON FUNDED DEBT, 1872
(Lines 1-6 in millions of dollars)

	1 If the actual profit of the promoters was $16,500,000	2 If the actual profit of the promoters was $13,000,000
1. Net earnings...........................	4.1	4.1
2. Adjusted net earnings..................	3.7	3.7
3. Interest on funded debt.................	5.1	5.1
4. Interest on funded debt on the assumption that the promoters limited themselves to the " justifiable " profit.....................	4.6	5.1
5. Interest on funded debt excluding the government bonds on the assumption that the promoters limited themselves to the " justiable " profit...........................	3.0	3.4
6. Interest on funded debt on the assumption that the promoters limited themselves to one-half of the " justifiable " profit.......	3.9	4.4
7. Line 3 as a percent of line 1.............	124	124
8. Line 4 as a percent of line 1.............	113	124
9. Line 5 as a percent of line 2.............	82	93
10. Line 6 as a percent of line 1.............	95	106

Sources and notes:

LINE 1. PRC, VIII, p. 4966.

LINE 2. *Ibid.*, pp. 4965-4966. The Act of 1864 required that one-half of the cost of government transportation be withheld from the railroad and applied to the payment of interest on the government bonds. *Cong. Globe, Append.*, 38th Cong., 1st Sess., p. 251. The adjusted net earnings are net earnings less the amount withheld by the government.

LINE 3. PRC, VIII, p. 4966.

LINE 4. Wilson, pp. 28, 595, 639. The figure in column 1 was derived on the assumption that the promoters took almost all of their " justifiable " profit in stock. This would have left the railroad with 5.4 million dollars in cash. With this sum the road could have eliminated its entire floating debt of 2.4 million dollars and 3.0/6.5 or 46 percent of its income bonds. The figure in column 1 is the interest on the remaining securities. The figure in column 2 was derived in a similar manner.

LINE 5. *Ibid.* The figure in column 1 was derived on the basis of the same assumption as was made in line 4. In this case, however, the entire government bond issue as well as the floating debt and 46 percent of the issue of income bonds are subtracted from the total debt of the company. The figure in column 1 is the interest on the remaining securities. The figure in column 2 was derived in a similar manner.

LINE 6. *Ibid.* The figure in column 1 was derived on the assumption that the promoters took one-half of the "justifiable" profit and all of their capital in stock. This left the railroad with 10.5 million dollars in cash and in stock taken at 30. With this sum the railroad could have eliminated its entire floating debt, all of its income bonds and 33 percent of its land-grant bonds. The figure in column 1 is the interest on the remaining securities. The figure in column 2 was derived in a similar manner.

floating debt and reduced the amount of its income bonds outstanding by about one-third. But, as shown in Table VI, even after this reduction of debt, the road would have been left with an interest burden which in 1872 [101] exceeded the net earnings of the road by 13 percent. And if the actual profit of the promoters was only 13.0 million dollars, the limitation on profit would have left the road with an interest burden that came to 124 percent of the net earnings of the road. Indeed, if the promoters, in a great burst of generosity, limited themselves to but *one-half* of the "justifiable" profit, the interest charge would still have ranged between 95 and 106 percent of the net earnings of the road.

It appears, then, that even a drastic reduction in profit of the promoters would not have produced a satisfactory interest-earnings ratio. This surprising result is not difficult to explain. Risk increased not only the supply price of equity capital but also that of loan capital. The railroad was forced to sell its bonds at large discounts. Although the question of whether the road would be completed was no longer really in doubt after 1867, the investing public obviously still had reservations concerning the earning capacity of the Union Pacific. The inability of the company to market its bonds at par inflated the bonded debt by 10.6 million dollars—two-thirds of the maximum profit of the promoters—and added close to a million dollars to the annual interest burden.[102]

In the long run the Union Pacific's ability to meet the interest charges on the government bonds proved to be as important as its ability to meet the charges on its own securities. It was the unbearable weight of its obligations to the government that finally forced the road into receivership in 1893.[103] However,

[101] It was on the basis of the company's position in 1872 that the Wilson committee charged that the profiteering of the promoters had brought the road to the brink of bankruptcy. Wilson, pp. XIX-XXII.

[102] *Ibid.*, p. 639.

[103] Stuart Daggett, *Railroad Reorganization* (Boston and New York: Houghton, Mifflin, 1908), pp. 238-57.

the railroad was not obliged to pay the interest on the government bonds in 1872.[104]   The imminent threat of bankruptcy to which the Wilson committee referred arose from the inadequate spread between the interest charges on the company's own securities and the earnings available to meet these charges. Limitation of the profit of the promoters to the " justifiable " amount would not have alleviated this threat either. The interest on the company's securities would still have ranged between 82 and 93 percent of the adjusted net earnings of the road. Such a narrow spread could hardly have insured the company's ability " to perform its important public functions without interruption in times of commercial disaster." Thus, regardless of whether one chooses to think of them as " daring innovators " or as " unmitigated cheats," the promoters cannot be held responsible for either the long or the short run financial instability of the Union Pacific. The responsibility must be placed at another door—the door of Congress.

The Union Pacific emerged as an unstable organization because the men who authored the Acts of 1862 and 1864 failed to understand the essence of the problem of premature enterprise. It was not only the amount of the capital needed to construct the Pacific road, but the risk attached to capital so invested that had prevented the building of the road under private auspices. Private businessmen had not built such a line because the expected profit (in the mathematical sense) was too low to justify the investment. While the Act of 1862 reduced the amount of private equity capital needed to finance the Union Pacific, it did not, in any way, free the prospective purchaser of stock from the risk of losing his investment. Quite the contrary, the particular form of government aid projected in the Act increased the risk to equity capital by saddling the road with a large bonded debt.

The Act of 1864 did little, if anything, to induce investors to purchase the stock of the Union Pacific. The clause permitting the railroad to issue its own first-mortgage bonds doubled the debt that equity had to carry, thus greatly increasing

---

[104] The government claimed that the Acts of 1862 and 1864 required the road to pay the interest on the government bonds on an annual basis. However, the Supreme Court decided against the government. The dispute is discussed in Haney, II, *op. cit.*, pp.85-88.

the risk to prospective stock purchasers.[105] At the same time this clause invited the entry of speculative promoters of the type associated with the Credit Mobilier. By allowing the road to issue its own first-mortgage bonds, Congress created a situation in which clever manipulators, willing to hazard very great risk, could foresee the possibility of reaping a fortune great enough to tempt them into taking up the enterprise. Indeed, under the Acts of 1862 and 1864 this was the only basis upon which private business could be induced to build the road. The outcome that the Wilson committee so much deplored was not the result of an unfortunate but avoidable accident that allowed the project to fall into the hands of " heartless speculators." The final outcome—the enervation of the Union Pacific—was built into the Acts of 1862 and 1864 by a Congress that failed to understand the implications of the risk that the investing public attached to the construction of a Pacific railroad.[106]

---

[105] It is true that the clause also increased the potential return to equity by increasing its " leverage." However, the complete failure of the stock subscription campaign of 1865 (see p. 58, above) suggests that in the minds of investors the greater leverage did not compensate for the increase in the risk that had to be borne by stockholders.

[106] With respect to the risk confronting prospective stockholders of the Union Pacific, the Act of 1864 was no better than the Act of 1862. However, with respect to its ability to actually bring about the construction of a road, the Act of 1864 was infinitely superior. The Union Pacific would not have been built under the earlier act; it was built under the later one. The Act of 1864 met the minimum price demanded by private promoters for the risk they had to bear. This was the most fundamental distinction between the two enactments.

CHAPTER IV

THE QUESTIONS OF PUBLIC POLICY

If sharp-sighted individual enterprise cannot be tempted to undertake it, then it certainly would be a most unprofitable and unwise undertaking for Government.

Representative Garrit Smith

Our population would be increased, our resources developed, and the continent covered with people and States from the Atlantic to the Pacific. Our wealth would be more than doubled; so would our products. A new impulse would be given to our agriculture, manufacturing, mining, commercial and navigating interests.

Senator William M. Gwin

Upon the hypothesis of the Senator from Vermont, this Government should build the road if it costs $100,000,000, and then spend $5,000,000 a year to run the road. A better proposition has been advanced here in this bill. It is proposed that the Government shall advance $60,000,000, or, rather, their bonds at thirty years as the road is completed in the course of a series of years. . . .

Senator James A. McDougall

Most contemporary accounts of the Union Pacific neglect the policy questions posed by government intervention in the building of the road. The slight is odd both because these questions were earnestly debated by Congress and the public for over 19 years and because the construction and subsequent operation of the road provide abundant data for testing the decisions finally reached by Congress. This curious treatment of the most massive enterprise sponsored by the American government during the nineteenth century appears to be due to an uncritical acceptance of the findings of the Wilson committee. The central thesis of the Congressional inquisitors was that the prostration of the Union Pacific was completely explained by the pernicious practices of the promoters. A " road built in accordance with the act of Congress," the inquisitors insisted, would have been a " strong," " solvent," " profitable," " powerful " business institution.[1] Thus, in accepting

[1] Wilson, pp. XXI, 558-59.

91

the findings of the Wilson committee, historians have relied on material that diverted attention from the policy decisions of Congress, that reduced the problems spawned by premature construction to a matter of personal morality.

However, if the thesis that profiteering was the root cause of the prostration of the Union Pacific is rejected, if the enervation of the road was inherent in the Acts of 1862 and 1864, the questions of public economic policy blurred by the Wilson committee spring back into focus. First, should the Union Pacific Railroad have been built prematurely; that is, should the government have intervened to bring about the construction of a road that would not have been undertaken by unaided private enterprise? Second, given the decision to intervene, what method of construction and financing would have been most efficient?

THE SOCIAL RATE OF RETURN

Properly conceived, the rate of return on the capital invested in the Union Pacific can be used as a basis for evaluating the economic wisdom of the government's decision to intervene in the building of a Pacific road. If the rate of return on the capital invested in the building of the Union Pacific was less than the market rate of return, then the Congressional decision was, on economic grounds, clearly a blunder. On the other hand, a rate of return that equalled the market rate of return would not necessarily validate the action taken by Congress. It would indicate that the Union Pacific was only one of a number of equally profitable investments that could have been undertaken at the time. Under this circumstance government intervention would have added nothing to the economic development of the country; it would merely have substituted one particular enterprise for some other enterprise of equal importance. The name of economic development may be invoked only if it can be shown that the rate of return on the Union Pacific investment *exceeded* the market rate of return. Indeed, the greater the margin by which the return on the capital so invested exceeded the market rate of return, the more confidence one would tend to have in the validity of the government decision to intervene.

It might be argued that profitability—the rate of return on an investment—is too narrow a criterion to be used for evaluating an investment decision when the objective is not private gain but national economic growth. Some of the most ardent proponents of a Pacific road strongly doubted its earning capacity. Senator Henry Wilson thought the idea that the Union Pacific would be able to earn enough to repay its debt to the government was " as visionary as anything that ever entered the brain of man." Nonetheless, he was prepared to " sink $100,000,000 to build the road " that would open up the " central regions of this continent " and " connect the people of the Pacific and Atlantic." [2] Senator Daniel Clark, who listed himself as a staunch supporter of a Pacific road, believed that " if the good God were to make the road for you, right through, you could not form a company in the country today that would run it without failure." [3] And Representative James Campbell saw no contradiction between his insistence that the project of a Pacific railroad would have to be " abandoned forever " unless it were heavily aided by the government and his prediction that the railroad would do more toward extending commerce and civilization over the continent " than any other enterprise of modern times." [4] To the proponents of the Acts of 1862 and 1864, the Union Pacific was, then, an investment that was of great *strategic* importance for the growth of the economy even though the company itself might earn less than the market rate of return on the capital required for its construction.

But what exactly is an investment that is unprofitable to the investing firm and yet is strategically important to the growth of the economy? [5] From the point of view of a firm, an unprofitable investment is one which increases the value of the product of the firm by a sum which is less than would have been achieved, on the average, if the same amount of capital had been applied elsewhere. In other words, if only the investing firm is considered, the substitution of an unprofitable investment for a profitable one is equivalent to a decrease in

[2] *Cong. Globe*, 37th Cong., 2d Sess., pp. 2754, 2758.
[3] *Ibid.*, p. 2788.
[4] *Ibid.*, pp. 1580, 1912.
[5] Economic growth is taken to mean an increase in national income per capita.

per capita national income. This implies that an investment which is unprofitable for the firm can be *strategically* important for the growth of the economy—for the increase in per capita income—only if it simultaneously serves to increase the productivity of labor and capital in firms[6] other than the one in which the investment is made; that is, only if there are firms which benefit from the investment but which do not have to pay for these benefits. In such cases the receipts of the investing firm do not reflect the full social value of the investment. The existence of these unpaid benefits is a necessary condition for an investment to be unprofitable for a firm and still serve to increase per capita income. Thus, investments which are privately unprofitable but which are strategically important for the growth of the economy involve not one but two rates of return—a private rate and a social rate. The private rate is based on the increase in the value of the product of the firm attributable to the given investment. The social rate is based on the increase in the value of the product of all firms[7] attributable to the investment. Clearly, it is on the basis of the social rate of return on the capital invested in the Union Pacific that the Congressional decision to intervene must be evaluated.

The fact that the Union Pacific tottered on the brink of bankruptcy suggests that the road was an unprofitable venture. This suggestion might seem to be supported by an examination of the ratio of the net earnings to the book value of the Union Pacific for the decade 1870-1879.[8] As shown in Table VII, this ratio varied from a low of 2.6 percent to a high of 6.9 percent, the average for the entire decade being 5.1 percent. And this over a span of years during which the average yield on the best grade of corporate bonds fluctuated between five and seven percent.[9] However, Table VII sheds little light on the economic

---

[6] As used here, the word " firms " includes the government and households as well as formally organized businesses.

[7] See note 6, above.

[8] Previous writers have based comments concerning the profitability of the Union Pacific investment on such an examination.

[9] Frederick R. Macaulay, *Some Theoretical Problems Suggested by the Movement of Interest Rates, Bond Yields and Stock Prices in the United States Since 1869* (New York: Nat. Bur. of Eco. Research, 1938), pp. A145-A147.

Judgement on the profitability or unprofitability of the Union Pacific investment requires a knowledge of the average rate of return on alternative investments. A

TABLE VII

THE RATE OF RETURN ON THE BOOK VALUE OF THE UNION PACIFIC
(In current dollars. 000 omitted)

	Year	1 Book value of the road	2 Net earnings	3 Column 2 as a percent of column 1
1.	1870	106,763	2,777	2.6
2.	1871	112,397	3,921	3.5
3.	1872	112,002	4,092	3.7
4.	1873	111,621	5,223	4.7
5.	1874	112,844	5,425	4.8
6.	1875	115,768	6,452	5.6
7.	1876	115,356	7,477	6.5
8.	1877	115,019	7,152	6.2
9.	1878	114,698	7,951	6.9
10.	1879	114,187	7,726	6.8
11.	Average rate of return on book value for the ten year period			5.1

Sources and notes:

COLUMN 1. Henry V. Poor, " The Pacific Railroad," *North American Review,* CXXVIII (July, 1879), p. 676.

COLUMN 2. PRC, VIII, p. 5266.

LINE 11. The average is constructed by dividing the sum of column 2 by the sum of column 1.

wisdom of the Congressional decision to build a Pacific road. The denominators of the ratios in column 3 include more than the cash expenditure on the construction of the Union Pacific. They also include the profit of the promoters and the discount on the company's bonds. Moreover, Table VII gives net

series giving the average rate of return on investments of comparable duration made at the same time that the Union Pacific investment was made, would provide one standard. The real annual rate of return on an 1869 purchase of high grade bonds provides another standard. When the average monthly high and low yields for 1869 are deflated by the Snyder-Tucker index, the resulting figures suggest that the real rate of return on an 1869 purchase of such bonds varied between 6.42 and 9.68 percent over the decade from 1870 to 1879. *Ibid.* Still another standard is the ratio of total earnings to the price of common stock. From 1871 through 1879 the average earnings-price ratio for all common stock on the New York Stock Exchange varied between 6.91 and 10.02 percent. The average for the nine year period was 8.86 percent. Alfred Cowles, 3rd, and associates, *Common-Stock Indexes* (2nd ed.; Bloomington, Indiana: Principia Press, 1939), p. 404. Despite their limitations, these series provide at least a rough basis for making the necessary judgement.

earnings in current dollars. The period from 1870 to 1879 was one of sharply declining prices. Thus the real net earnings of the road were considerably greater than the figures of Table VII indicate.

TABLE VIII

THE RATE OF RETURN ON THE CASH EXPENDITURE ON CONSTRUCTION
(In constant dollars of 1869. 000 omitted)

	Year	1 Accumulated expenditure on construction	2 Net earnings adjusted for depreciation	3 Column 2 as a percent of column 1
1.	1870	53,060	2,240	4.2
2.	1871	53,950	3,610	6.7
3.	1872	54,830	3,670	6.7
4.	1873	55,230	5,020	9.1
5.	1874	55,490	5,490	9.9
6.	1875	55,620	7,000	12.6
7.	1876	55,630	8,760	15.7
8.	1877	59,160	8,670	14.7
9.	1878	59,160	10,530	17.8
10.	1879	59,160	10,370	17.5
11.	Average rate of return on construction expenditure for the ten year period................			11.6

Sources and notes:

COLUMN 1. Above, pp. 71-72; PRC, VIII, pp. 5046-48, 5053, 5068-72, 5098-5100. The cost of the road in current dollars through 1869 was $51,978,361. Assuming cash expenditures on construction for the years 1865-1869 were proportional to the miles of road constructed in each year, the annual expenditure on construction was $1,764,000 in 1865, $12,001,000 in 1866, $11,729,000 in 1867, $17,082,000 in 1868 and $6,736,000 in 1869. These figures were then deflated by the Snyder-Tucker price index with the base shifted to 1869. The sum of the resulting figures—$49,310,000—is the cost of building the road through the year 1869 in constant dollars. The entries of column I were obtained by adding to the last figure, construction expenditures for each year from 1870 through 1879 as given in PRC, VIII, after converting these annual construction expenditures into constant dollars of 1869.

COLUMN 2. Above, pp. 71-72; Sen. Exec. Docs. No. 69, 49th Cong., 1st Sess. (2336), p. 54. The figures for net earnings in current dollars given in PRC, VIII, p. 5266 were converted into net earnings in constant dollars of 1869 by deflating with the Snyder-Tucker index. An adjustment for depreciation was necessary since the Union Pacific did not deduct depreciation charges from its net earnings. However, replacement of rails and ties were charged to operating expenses as they were made. Wilson, pp. 216-18. Since the average length of life of an iron rail in the United States at this time was about ten years (Sir Lowthian Bell, *The Iron Trade of the United Kingdom Compared with that of the Other Chief Iron-making Nations*—London: British Iron Trade Association,

1886—, p. 143), it may be assumed that all of the rails used in the original construction of the road were replaced by 1879. This still leaves depreciation charges on structures, equipment, etc. unaccounted for. The neglected charges were estimated in the following manner: *Sen. Exec. Docs.* No. 69 contains an estimate, prepared by J. L. Williams, of the cost of the road. Williams allocated 38.342 percent of the cost of the road to structures, grading, bridges, tunnels, etc.; 43.776 percent to track; and 17.882 percent to equipment. Applying these weights to the depreciable cost of the road through 1872 ($57,028,272 less $4,061,454), the estimated cost of structures, etc. is $16,874,000 and equipment is $9,739,000. Assuming the former depreciated over 50 years and the latter over 20, the annual depreciation costs neglected by the company are about $824,000. Column 2, then, gives the net earnings of the road in dollars of 1869 less the estimated neglected depreciation charges.

LINE 11. The average is constructed by dividing the sum of column 2 by the sum of column 1.

Table VIII corrects these and other errors. This table shows an annual ratio of real net earnings adjusted for depreciation to accumulated real cash expenditure on construction that varied between 4.2 and 17.5 percent. The average for the decade was 11.6 percent. These figures lead to a startling conclusion. The Union Pacific was premature by mistake! It was premature because private investors expected it to be unprofitable. But their expectations were based on an incorrect evaluation of the course of economic development. In actual fact the road was a highly profitable venture that should have been taken up by unaided private enterprise. Interestingly enough, only in the halls of Congress did one find a sizable proportion of individuals who, like Senator James H. Lane of Kansas, stubbornly predicted that the completed Union Pacific would be " one of the great paying thoroughfares of the world." [10] This fact might be taken as an indication that Congress perceived the true state of nature while private businessmen had failed to do so. The ability of Congress to have foreseen a large profit for the owners of the Union Pacific would, even in the absence of unpaid benefits, tend to justify the decision to intervene. Yet, despite the appeal of the idea, there is no real evidence that the nation's political leaders possessed a superior vision. The optimism of Lane, and others, was probably more a matter of political expediency—rhetoric calculated to create a favorable atmosphere for the promotion of the road—than the expression of a personal conviction. At any rate, neither

[10] *Cong. Globe*, 37th Cong., 2d Sess., p. 2788.

Lane, nor McDougall, nor Latham, nor several of the other optimists availed themselves of the opportunity to buy shares in this "great paying thoroughfare." Their names are not among the ones on the list of the original subscribers to the Union Pacific.[11]

The case for government intervention rested on the conviction, held by businessmen and legislators alike, that the road would bring great social returns. The 11.6 percent figure cited above is the average *private* return on the construction expenditure. It does not include the unpaid benefits of the road—the increase in national income brought about by the road but which failed to be reflected in the company's net earnings. While the conception of the social rate of return is clear, the calculation of it involves considerable practical difficulty. Given the necessary data, aggregate analysis would provide the most direct method of determining the social rate. If there had existed a nation which had been the twin of the United States in every respect except that it had not built the Union Pacific, the social rate of return on the investment could be determined by first finding the differences in annual national income between the two countries over the life of the investment, and then finding the rate of discount which made the present value of these annual income differences equal to the amount of the investment. However, since the United States did not have such a national twin, this method of procedure is ruled out.

Alternative approaches involve the disaggregation of the increase in national income attributable to the Union Pacific. The net earnings of the road represent one part of the postulated increase in income. The rest is included under the heading of unpaid benefits. These unpaid benefits can be divided into four categories: (a) the increase in income, not reflected in the company's receipts, due to the opening up of lands in states through which the railroad passed; (b) the saving to private shippers in areas east of Omaha and west of Ogden City as a result of being able to utilize the Union Pacific for shipment to points beyond the territory traversed by the road at lower rates than would otherwise have prevailed; (c) the saving to the government as a result of being able to transport men, mail

[11] Wilson, pp. 740-42.

and material at low railroad rates instead of high wagon and steamship rates; (d) the saving to producers outside the immediate territory of the Union Pacific as a result of a better division of labor made possible by the existence of the railroad. The sum of these unpaid benefits plus the net earnings of the road, then, would provide the desired estimate of the total increase in income attributable to the Union Pacific.

Unfortunately the data needed to determine the unpaid benefits falling into categories (b), (c) and (d) are not available.[12] However, it is possible to obtain an approximate estimate of the unpaid benefits of category (a)—the increase in national income, not reflected in the Union Pacific's receipts, brought about by the increase in the productivity of labor and capital when utilized on the lands opened up for commercial exploitation by the railroad. This figure plus the net earnings of the road would be less than the increase in national income attributable to the Union Pacific. Nonetheless, it would convey some conception of the order of magnitude of the desired figure.

The basis for the estimate of the unpaid benefits of category (a) is the theory of rent.[13] In 1880 the value of all lands on a strip approximately 40 miles on each side of the Union Pacific from Omaha to Ogden was about $158,500,000 (in dollars of 1869). This figure is the capitalization of the amount

---

[12] In 1874 the government directors of the Union Pacific prepared an estimate of the government saving on the transportation of mail, men and military supplies attributable to the existence of the railroad. Basing themselves on statistics supplied by the Postmaster General and the Secretary of War, they concluded that the average annual saving over a two year period beginning June 30, 1872 was $1,894,894 in current dollars—or $2,114,685 in dollars of 1869. Extending the latter figure over the years from 1870 to 1879, the estimated saving to the government for the decade would be 21.1 million dollars.

These figures have been omitted from the body of the paper because the following dubious assumptions were explicitly or implicitly made by the directors in preparing their estimate: (1) The cost of transporting mail in 1872 by means other than railroads would have been the same cost that prevailed in 1860. (2) The amount of transportation purchased by the government was independent of changes in population and income both in the nation as a whole and in the area traversed by the Union Pacific. (3) The government demand for transportation was completely inelastic even over price changes of 360 percent.

These assumptions bias the directors' estimate by an indeterminable amount. *Sen. Exec. Docs.* No. 69, 49th Cong., 1st Sess. (2336), pp. 95-96; see also *H. Exec. Docs.* Nos. 151 and 169, 42d Cong., 3d Sess. (1567).

[13] All references connected with the calculation of the unpaid benefits of category (a) are given in the notes to Table IX.

by which the value of the annual product produced by labor and capital on these lands exceeded the value of the product of the same amount of labor and capital working on marginal land. If the railroad had not existed, the overwhelming bulk of the lands surrounding the Union Pacific would have been unusable and the labor and capital employed on them would have been employed elsewhere at either the intensive or extensive margins. Thus, if in 1880 the railroad had been suddenly removed, the annual loss in income to society would have been the decapitalized fall in the value of the lands on the 80 mile strip. Put more positively, the increase in national income due to the Union Pacific, but not reflected in its receipts, is the decapitalized value of the amount by which the actual value of the lands on the 80 mile strip exceeded the value that would have obtained if there had been no railroad.[14]

In 1860 the value of the lands in the 80 mile strip was about $4,370,000 (in dollars of 1869). This figure is the estimated value of the designated lands, given the labor and capital that existed in the United States in 1860. Since the quantity of labor and capital in the country increased during the decades that followed 1860, we would expect the value of the land in the 80 mile strip to have been somewhat higher than $4,370,000 in 1880 even if the Union Pacific had not been built.[15] Between 1860 and 1880 the value of all farm lands in the United States increased by 32.9 percent.[16] Therefore, it is reasonable to assume that even without the railroad, land values would have been 32.9 percent higher than they were 20 years earlier. Hence, the estimated value of the lands on the 80 mile strip in 1880 in the absence of the Union Pacific, given the labor and capital of 1880, is $5,800,000.[17]

[14] Cf. George J. Stigler, *The Theory of Price* (New York: Macmillan, 1954), p. 192.

[15] If more capital and labor were applied to the same amount of land then, *ceteris paribus*, the value of the marginal product of land, and hence the value of land, would rise. This in turn would cause more land to be drawn into use.

[16] Most of the land in use in the 80 mile strip in 1860 was farm land. The land in use would probably have continued to have been mainly farm land if there had been no railroad. Hence the comparison with the increase in value of all farm lands seems to be more appropriate than an urban-land or an all-land comparison.

[17] On the other hand, the average value of an acre of farm land in 1880 was almost the same as it had been two decades earlier. Farm lands averaged $25.51

The approximate increase in the value of land due to the railroad, then, was $152,700,000. If this figure is multiplied by a properly weighted average of the rates at which land rents in the relevant states were capitalized, the resulting figure—$15,630,000—is an estimate of the increase in national income in 1880 due to the productivity of labor and capital on the lands made available by the Union Pacific but not reflected in the company's receipts.[18] Column 3 of Table IX gives an estimate of this neglected increase in national income for the decade from 1870 through 1879. Adding these figures to the net earnings of the road, we find that the annual *social* rate of return on the capital expended on the construction of the road varied between 15.3 and 42.3 percent. The average for the decade was 29.9 percent. However, 29.9 percent is a minimum estimate of the social rate of return on the construction expenditure. The figure does not reflect the unpaid benefits of categories (b), (c) and (d), listed above.[19] Clearly, then, from a social point of view the Union Pacific was a most

per acre in 1860 and $25.75 in 1880 (in dollars of 1869). This suggests that there may have been a considerable increase in the quantity of available better land (either as a result of improved transportation or an advance in agricultural technology). If this was the case, the value of the land on the 80 mile strip might have remained unchanged between 1860 and 1880 despite the increase in labor and capital.

[18] The preceding analysis involved two implicit assumptions that should be made explicit. First, it was assumed that the rate of population growth in the nation as a whole would not have been affected by the absence of the Union Pacific. Secondly, it was assumed that the absence of the Union Pacific would not have altered the rate of capital accumulation.

The justification for the first assumption lies in the fact that while the increase in income due to the opening up of the lands in the 80 mile strip is large relative to the investment in the Union Pacific, it is infinitesimal (in the neighborhood of 0.15 of one percent) relative to national income in 1880. In view of this, it hardly seems likely that the absence of the railroad would have significantly altered any of the main variables upon which population growth is usually taken to depend.

Similarly, the amount of supramarginal land within the 80 mile strip was a small proportion of the total amount of supramarginal land in the country. Hence the absence of the Union Pacific would have had little influence on factor proportions—on which the rate of return to capital may be taken to depend—and, therefore, on the rate of capital accumulation.

[19] The building of the Union Pacific may have induced some external diseconomies. For example, the displacement of the Pony Express may have involved some uncompensated costs. If there were such uncompensated costs, their magnitude was probably quite small compared to the magnitude of the unpaid benefits.

profitable venture.[20] There can be little doubt that the government was economically justified in intervening to build a road that would not have been built by unaided private enterprise.

TABLE IX

ESTIMATED SOCIAL RETURN ON CONSTRUCTION EXPENDITURE
(In constant dollars of 1869. 000 omitted)

	Year	1 Accumulated expenditure on construction	2 Net earnings adjusted for depreciation	3 Increase in National Income due to Union Pacific but not reflected in company's earnings	4 Sum of columns 2 and 3	5 Column as a percent of column
1.	1870	53,060	2,240	5,860	8,100	15.3
2.	1871	53,950	3,610	6,840	10,450	19.4
3.	1872	54,830	3,670	7,810	11,480	20.9
4.	1873	55,230	5,020	8,790	13,810	25.0
5.	1874	55,490	5,490	9,770	15,260	27.5
6.	1875	55,620	7,000	10,740	17,740	31.9
7.	1876	55,630	8,760	11,720	20,480	36.8
8.	1877	59,160	8,670	12,700	21,370	36.1
9.	1878	59,160	10,530	13,670	24,200	40.9
10.	1879	59,160	10,370	14,650	25,020	42.3
11.	Average social rate of return for the ten year period............................					29.9

Sources and notes:

COLUMN 1.   See note to column 1 of Table VIII.

COLUMN 2.   See note to column 2 of Table VIII.

COLUMN 3.   The figures in this column represent estimates of the annual increase in national income due to the greater productivity of labor and capital on the lands made available by the Union Pacific not reflected in the net earnings of the company. The estimates were made in the following manner:

First, a list was made of all counties lying within a strip approximately 40 miles on each side of the railroad. These counties fell into four states: Nebraska, Utah, Wyoming and Colorado.

Second, the assessed value of the land plus improvements in these counties 1880 was obtained from U. S., Bureau of the Census, *Tenth Census of the United States, Valuation, Taxation and Public Indebtedness*, pp. 201-204, 212-14.

Third, the Census of 1880 gave not only the assessed value of the property in each state but also an estimate of the true value of the property (*Ibid.*, p. 12). This permitted the construction of a valuation adjustment factor for each state. These factors were 4.2501 for Nebraska, 4.6014 for Utah, 3.9642 for Wyoming and 3.2227 for Colorado. By multiplying the assessed value of the land plus improvements by the appropriate valuation adjustment factor, an estimate of the true value (in current dollars) of the land plus improvements was obtained.

---

[20] If the estimated annual savings to the government given in note 12, p. 99, above is added to the figures in column 4, Table IX, the average social rate of return for the decade becomes 33.7 percent.

Fourth, the value of improvements was separated from the value of the land by applying estimates of the ratio of the value of improvements to the value of real estate taken from the work of Professor Simon Kuznets. Kuznets estimated that for the United States as a whole in 1880 the value of farm improvements was 20 percent of the value of farm lands plus improvements. The value of improvements on non-farm land was 56.94 percent of the value of non-farm lands plus improvements (Simon Kuznets, *National Product Since 1869*—New York: Nat. Bur. of Eco. Research, 1946—, pp. 201-202). The average of these two ratios, weighted by the ratios of the value of farm and non-farm real estate to the value of all real estate in each of the states, yielded an " improvement-land " adjustment factor. One minus the " improvements-land " adjustment factor for each state gave a " land-improvement " factor for each state. The " land-improvements " factor multiplied by the true value of real estate (including improvements) produced the estimated true value of the land alone on the 80 mile strip. The resulting figures were then deflated by the Snyder-Tucker price index to give the value of the land in dollars of 1869.

Fifth, an estimate of the true value of the land (in dollars of 1869) on the same strip in 1860 was determined in a similar manner. The basic data for this estimate were taken from U. S., Bureau of the Census, *Eighth Census of the United States, Statistics of the United States*, pp. 295, 317-18. This figure was multiplied by the ratio of the value of all farm lands in 1880 to the value of all farm lands in 1860 (both numerator and denominator were expressed in dollars of 1869). (U. S., Bureau of the Census, *Eleventh Census of the United States, Report on the Statistics of Agriculture*, pp. 84-85.) The resulting figure— $5,800,000—is the estimate of the value that the lands in the 80 mile strip would have had in 1880 if there had been no railroad.

Sixth, the increase in the value of the land due to the railroad was obtained by subtracting the estimated value of the lands in 1880 without the railroad from the estimated actual value of the lands in 1880. The resulting calculation showed that the increase in land values in the selected counties was approximately $152,700,000 of which $105,070,000 was in Nebraska, $31,057,000 was in Utah, $10,785,000 was in Wyoming, and $5,832,000 was in Colorado.

Seventh, these figures were decapitalized by multiplying them by the mortgage rate of interest in the respective states. By states, the average mortgage rates of interest in 1880 were 8.82 percent in Nebraska, 13.46 percent in Utah, 14.22 percent in Wyoming, and 11.05 percent in Colorado. (U. S., Bureau of the Census, *Eleventh Census of the United States, Report on Real Estate Mortgages*, p. 248.) The sum of the resulting figures—$15,630,000—is the estimated neglected increase in national income for 1880.

Eighth, the estimates for the years 1870-1879 were obtained by interpolation on a straight line basis over the years from 1865 through 1880.

LINE 11. The average is constructed by dividing the sum of column 4 by the sum of column 1.

THE EFFICIENCY OF THE ACTS OF 1862 AND 1864

While the extremely high social rate of return tends to confirm the government's decision to build a Pacific road, it does not imply that the particular method of construction and financing chosen by Congress was a good one. It is not possible to assess the economic efficacy of the construction scheme projected by Congress without first establishing a criterion of efficiency on the basis of which the relative merit of alternative construction schemes might be evaluated. The criterion to be used in this examination is the cost of the road to the firm. The most efficient method of intervention, then, would have been the method which made the cost of building the road to the firm a minimum.

If the Union Pacific had been a riskless enterprise, the cost of the road to the company would have been approximately the cash that was actually expended on construction—$57,028,272 through 1872.[21] In this case the Union Pacific would not have been faced with "extra" charges for the service of the promoters or with premiums on borrowed money. However, the Union Pacific was a highly risky enterprise. In the light of the risks attached to the building of the road, the promoters were, as we have seen, "entitled" to a construction profit of 11.1 million dollars. To the company, then, necessary construction expenditures included not only such items as the cost of materials, payments to the various sub-contractors who did the actual work, legal and administrative expenses, etc., but also the "justifiable" profits of the promoters—the profit without which, under the Acts of 1862 and 1864, the indispensable

[21] Alley and several of the other promoters claimed that the speed at which the road was constructed increased the cost of the road by 25 percent (11.4 million dollars). Since rapid construction was motivated largely by the desire of the promoters to obtain government bonds and lands that would otherwise have fallen to the Central Pacific, it might be argued that under a construction plan that held construction down to a normal speed the social cost of the road would only have been 45.6 million dollars (57.0 less 11.4 million dollars). This argument overlooks the fact that slow construction would also have involved an "extra" cost. The "extra" cost in this case is the present value of the income that would have been lost if it took, say, eight years instead of four years to build the road. If it is assumed that the earnings of the road during the period of construction were proportional to the number of miles of track completed, and if it is also assumed that the rate of increase in the earnings of the firm after construction was completed would have been the same under both slow and rapid construction, then it can be shown that the present value of the net earnings of the firm that would have been lost as a result of slow construction would have been at least 15.6 million dollars. Hence to the firm, the cost of slow construction would have exceeded the cost of rapid construction by at least 4.2 million dollars. If the present value of the income lost to society is considered, the case for rapid construction becomes overwhelming. Wilson, p. 560; PRC, VIII, p. 5266; Poor, *North American Review, loc. cit.*, p. 668.

services of the promoters could not have been secured. Hence, from the point of view of the firm, necessary construction expenditures were 68.1 million dollars.

Even this last figure does not give the full cost of the road to the company. For, to the company, the cost of the road depended not only on the necessary construction expenditure but also on how much the company had to pay for the funds it needed to cover these expenditures. The cost of funds is usually given as the rate of interest. However, it is also possible to measure the cost of funds by the present value of the interest and principal payments to which a borrower commits himself when he makes a loan. The present value approach poses the problem of the rate at which future interest and principal payments should be discounted. The solution to the problem is suggested by the fact that the cost of a loan to a borrower is always a conditional cost. The cost of a loan is, say, six percent, or $60 per year on each $1,000 advanced, *if, and only if,* the borrower fulfills his contractual obligation. However, given the condition that the borrower will meet these obligations, the future payments are certain and the proper rate of discount is the market rate of interest. In other words, the *conditional* cost of funds to the Union Pacific was the present value of the payments it pledged to its suppliers of funds, discounted at the market rate of interest—6.02 percent.

The money the Union Pacific needed to meet its construction charges was obtained in three ways. Approximately 11.0 million was secured through the company's sale of stock; 27.1 million dollars was provided by the government; the remaining 30.0 million dollars was procured through loans from private individuals or firms. Of the 30.0 million dollars, the Union Pacific acquired 23.7 million dollars by selling its first-mortgage bonds. But for every $871.57 the company received on this security it pledged to make future payments with a present value of $997.25. To the company, then, the cost of 23.7 million dollars was 27.1 million dollars.[22] The remaining 6.3 million dollars needed by the road was obtained by selling income bonds. On

---

[22] This figure neglects the fact that the first-mortgage bonds were gold bonds and that gold was at a premium in the period during which the bonds were sold. Wilson, pp. 28, 619-28; *Commercial and Financial Chronicle,* XII (January 7, 1871), p. 21; above, p. 72 and note 90, p. 82.

this security the company committed itself to payments with a present value of $1,106.35 for every $700.23 advanced, the cost of 6.3 million dollars being approximately 10.0 million dollars.[23] If the premium the Union Pacific had to pay on the borrowed funds is added to the other construction charges, the cost of the road to the firm becomes 75.1 million dollars.[24]

During the course of the long debate on a Pacific road, both legislators and private citizens offered a host of schemes for government intervention, alternative to the one actually chosen by Congress. These proposals fall into three groups. The first group consists of proposals for " privately " owned roads, aided only by a government grant of land. The Gwin bill, one of the most prominent of these schemes, projected a grant of alternate sections of land for 40 miles on each side of the railroad.[25] If this plan had been adopted, the Union Pacific would have received lands which were worth approximately $76,350,000 in 1880. This implies that if in 1869 investors had known the 1880 value of the lands, the most the railroad could have obtained on these lands would have been $40,100,000. Since the Union Pacific received one-half of this amount of land under the Act of 1864, the most the additional land offered by the Gwin bill could have been worth was $20,050,000—about 7.1 million dollars less than the value of the bonds the Union Pacific received from the government under the Acts of 1862 and 1864. However, this estimate of the value of these additional lands is much too favorable. When the Union Pacific mortgaged its lands in 1869, it received only 6.1 million dollars; [26] and this on land which, in general, was more valuable than the additional lands of the Gwin bill, since it was located closer to the railroad. These considerations suggest that the

[23] The income bonds were three year bonds that paid ten percent on the face value. *Ibid*.

[24] Under all of the plans considered in this chapter, the cost of the road to society would have been approximately the same—approximately 57.0 million dollars, the cash expenditure on construction. The cost of the road to the company is important for two reasons. First, it has a bearing on the post-construction financial stability of the firm. The greater the cost of the road to the company, the greater the bonded debt, and therefore, the fixed charges the completed Union Pacific had to carry. Secondly, it has a bearing on the question of equity—i. e., on the distribution of the social saving among individuals. See note 32, 110, below.

[25] The details of the Gwin bill are given on pp. 33-35, above.

[26] Wilson, p. 639.

railroad would not have received more than 6.1 million dollars in loans based on the additional lands—21.0 million dollars less than it received in government bonds. Even the Whitney bill, the most lavish of all the land-grant schemes, would not have closed the gap. Under the terms of the Whitney bill, the Union Pacific would have received additional lands of 41,360 square miles; [27] yet the funds the road would have been able to raise on such a dukedom would still have been at least 14.9 million dollars less than the proceeds of the government bond issue. Moreover, on the money borrowed on these lands, the road would have paid not six but over ten percent in interest. Hence even the most lavish of the land-grant schemes was clearly inferior to—less efficient than—the one actually adopted by Congress.

The second group of alternatives consists of the type of proposal that held the center of the stage during the years from 1852 through 1860—the type of proposal embodied in the Douglas, Weller, Rusk and McDougall bills.[28] Like the purely land-grant schemes, all of these measures would have been less efficient than the plan under which the Union Pacific was actually constructed. In all of them the amount of government bond aid that would have fallen to the Union Pacific was less than half of the amount the Union Pacific actually received. Moreover, these bills did not provide for the issuance of first-mortgage bonds so that the road would have had to raise the 23.7 million dollars brought in by the first-mortgage bonds on inferior securities. Finally, since most of these bills contained provisos for the eventual surrender of the road to the government, the risk to equity capital would have been even greater than the risk that obtained under the Acts of 1862 and 1864.

Of all the schemes that gained prominence during the long debate over a Pacific road, only three could have been more efficient than the one under which the Union Pacific was actually built. These three schemes constitute the final group of alternatives. The "Boston Plan," put forth by P. P. F. DeGrand, suggested the establishment of a corporation to which the government would have loaned $98,000,000 and private individuals

[27] H. Repts. No. 140, 31st Cong., 1st Sess. (583), p. 44. The details of the Whitney bill are given on pp. 28-32, above.
[28] For the details of these bills see pp. 35-37, above.

would have subscribed $2,000,000. In return for its loan the government was to have received six percent interest and half of the stock.[29] If these amounts had been divided between the Central Pacific and the Union Pacific in proportion to the length of each road, the Union Pacific would have received 57.0 million dollars from the government and 1.2 million dollars from private subscriptions. In other words, under this scheme, the Union Pacific would have received all of the capital it needed for the construction of the road from the government at six percent. For the private investors there would no longer have been a risk of inadequate funds (assuming they had the same information on construction costs that Durant and his associates had in 1863). Moreover, for their investment of 1.2 million dollars, the private subscribers stood to gain 50 percent of all of the net earnings of the road over the interest on the government loan. Under such provisions as these the cost of constructing the road would probably have been quite close to the cash expenditure on construction—$57,028,272.

The second potentially efficient plan proposed that a private firm build the road, but that the government guarantee the firm five or six percent—i. e., approximately the prevailing market rate of return—on the cost of construction.[30] This plan would have shifted all of the risk to the government. Hence, the company would have had no trouble in obtaining all of the funds that it needed through the sale of stock. Indeed, if the firm had issued $57,000,000 of stock, the stock would have sold above par. For such stock would have been better than a government bond. The least the firm would have earned on its investment was the market rate of interest; and there was always the possibility that the road could have earned a great deal more.

The third plan called on the government to build the road itself.[31] Since the government could have obtained all of the funds that it needed at the market rate of interest, the cost of the road to the firm would have been the cash expenditure on construction—$57,028,272.

Under all of the plans in the third group, the firm would have received all of the funds needed for contruction at six

[29] Russel, op. cit., pp. 46-47.

[30] One such plan is given by Bancroft, VII, op. cit., p. 502.

[31] The details of one such scheme, the Wilson bill, are given on pp. 37-38, above.

percent. Hence, the fixed charges on the completed road would have been a minimum. The completed Union Pacific would have emerged as the "strong," "solvent," "powerful" business institution that the Wilson committee wanted it to be. However, in each case this blissful state of events would have been due to the fact that the government intervened between the firm and the investing public, using the credit of the government to obtain funds from the public at six percent and then supplying these funds to the firm at the same market rate of interest. In other words, the cost of construction would have been a minimum only because the government shifted the risk from private investors to itself. This type of intervention raises another question of efficiency. Why should the government have been willing to provide funds to the firm at six percent when the rate of return demanded by private investors was two, three and four times at great? Would not a government advance at such low rates have represented a misallocation of capital? There were at least two good reasons for a government advance of funds at a rate well below the rate demanded by private suppliers of funds. First, in calculating the rate of return that they should demand on their money, private investors had to take into account the risk that the Union Pacific might fail because it could not obtain *all* of the funds needed to complete the road. If the government had built the road, or had supplied the funds needed to build the road, this risk would not have existed. Secondly, private investors evaluated the Union Pacific on the basis of the expected *private* earnings of the road. For the government the relevant consideration was the expected *social* earnings. Since the common contention of both government figures and private individuals was that a Pacific road would be socially profitable, the expected social earnings must have been at least equal to the market rate of return.

While all of the plans that make up the last group of proposals would have drastically reduced the cost of funds to the firm, they were not all equally feasible or equally desirable from the point of view of the government. Under the Boston plan the government was to supply 98 percent of the money but it would have received considerably less than 98 percent of the profit. The guaranteed profit plan also had an Achilles heel;

it contained a tendency to waste. Since the company was guaranteed six percent on the cost of the road, profit maximization might have acted as a spur to increasing rather than decreasing the cost of construction. These considerations suggest that from the point of view of the government, government construction might have been the most desirable means of obtaining a Pacific road. The great objection to a government enterprise arose from a distaste for the involvement of the government in business. However, the government could have minimized this objection by selling the Union Pacific to private individuals shortly after the road was completed—say, in 1875 or 1876—at its capitalized value. If the last course of action had been followed, society would have reaped the same social gain that it did under the Acts of 1862 and 1864; but, in addition, the Union Pacific would have been a sound business institution and the government would have realized a tidy profit on the transaction.[32]

*   *   *

The building of the Union Pacific is more than an episode in history; it a great American myth. The story of how this proud enterprise was ruined by rapacious promoters is as integral a part of the myth as the romantic versions of the explorations that preceded the road, the battles with the Indians, the armies of men pounding an Anvil Chorus across the plains, the race to the finish and the driving of the golden spike. Those who cherish the myth in all its aspects need not be distraught because of the rummaging of scholars. Once formed, myths are sturdy things; they can withstand the findings of a dozen documented studies. The myth of the Union Pacific is probably invincible. The Indians will continue to be routed, the golden spike will continue to be driven, and the road will continue to be ruined by unscrupulous promoters in story and song, regardless of what is written in history books.

[32] This scheme would also have had important equity effects. If the road had been built by the government and then had been sold at its capitalized value, the profit that was reaped by the promoters and by those who bought Union Pacific bonds at a discount would have accrued to the government. This profit would have increased the income of the government, thus decreasing, *ceteris paribus*, the government's need for taxes. Hence the distribution of the social saving brought about by the road would have been wider in this case than was true under the Acts of 1862 and 1864.

APPENDIX A

THE BOND TRANSACTIONS OF 1869-1870

In 1869 and 1870 the trustees of the Ames and Davis contracts engaged in certain bond transactions. This appendix examines the relationship between these transactions and the upper and lower limits of the profit of the promoters given on pages 69-71, above.

1). The Union Pacific issued land-grant bonds and income bonds in 1869 in order to obtain funds needed for the purchase of rolling stock, and for the retirement of accumulated debts—totaling between 13 and 14 million dollars.[1]

2). During the latter part of 1869 the market for the securities of the Union Pacific weakened considerably. First-mortgage bonds which were quoted at 103 in February, 1869, dropped to 88 in July and to 80 in October.[2] The average price of first-mortgage bonds during the last two and one-half months of 1869 was 82.6; the average price of the land-grant bonds was 56.2.

On January 15, 1870 land-grant bonds were at 55⅛ (first-mortgage bonds were at 81¾). Two weeks later the land-grants suddenly jumped 12 points to 67½. They edged up to 73 by March 26, 1870. March 26th is the first date on which there is a quotation on income bonds; the price was 84½. Between April 30th and July 9th, land-grant bonds ranged between 76 and 77, income bonds between 84 and 87. During July, both bonds began a steady downward movement. By December 10, 1870, land-grant bonds had fallen to 54 and the income bonds to 33½.

As noted above, there were no quotations on income bonds prior to March 26, 1870. However, the relative movements

---

[1] Wilson, pp. 27, 47-48.

[2] All quotations on the prices of Union Pacific securities are taken from the *Commercial and Financial Chronicle* of the relevant date.

111

of land-grants bonds and income bonds during the rest of 1870 indicates that income bonds were the more volatile security. Income bonds ran higher than land-grants when the market for Union Pacific securities was relatively strong, and lower than land-grants in a weak market. This suggests that during the period from October, 1869 through February, 1870, when land-grants were selling in the fifties and sixties, income bonds were probably selling in the sixties or below.

3). The seven trustees apparently agreed to buy several million dollars worth of income bonds from the Union Pacific in order to provide " money to meet the pressing necessities of the company." [3] Crane stated that the trustees paid 60 cents on the dollar for these securities.[4] Altogether, the trustees bought bonds with a face value of $5,840,000. The purchases were as follows: October 30, 1869—$1,700,000; January 31, 1870—$2,201,000; February 28, 1870—$1,139,000.[5]

For the same reason, the trustees also bought $275,000 in land-grant bonds at 55 and $275,000 in first-mortgage bonds at 85. The date of purchase is not indicated. Presumably they were also bought during the period of time when the market was weak.[6]

4). Sometimes during 1870, the trustees sold the $5,840,000 of income bonds and $11,680,000 of Union Pacific stock to the stockholders of the Credit Mobilier for $4,672,000; that is, the trustees sold blocks of securities to the promoters consisting of one bond and 20 shares of stock at $800 per block.[7]

5). What significance does this transaction have in the setting of an upper limit on the range of the possible profits of the promoters? The Union Pacific stock that was distributed with the income bonds is already included in the upper profit limit given on p. 70 and need not be considered further here. However, it is necessary to consider the significance of the bond sale *per se*. The evaluation of this transaction is somewhat complicated by the lack of definite information as to the dates on which the trustees sold the bonds to the promoters.

[3] Wilson, p. 645.
[4] *Ibid.*, p. 631.
[5] *Ibid.*, pp. 627-28.
[6] *Ibid.*, pp. 633, 645.
[7] *Ibid.*, pp. XVI, 630, 645.

If the trustees sold the bonds as soon as they received them, there was no profit on the transaction. The trustees bought the bonds at 60 and sold them when they were worth 60. However, for each bond they sold, the trustees received 80. The additional 20, then, was a *de facto* increase in the amount of capital supplied by the stockholders of the Credit Mobilier. In other words, if the trustees sold the bonds as soon as they received them, the transaction was equivalent to a $1,168,000 increase in the investment of the promoters.

6). The Wilson committee held that the average value of the income bonds at the time the trustees disposed of them was 80.[8] If this price was correct, the entire $4,672,000 received by the trustees was a payment for the income bonds, and the $11,680,000 of Union Pacific stock was, as the Wilson committee claimed, in effect, given to the promoters who made the purchase as a stock dividend. In this case there was no *de facto* addition to the venture capital of the promoters. Instead, there was a gain of $1,168,000 on the transaction since the trustees sold each bond for $200 more than they paid for it. The upper limit given on p. 70 excludes this gain. The rationale for the exclusion is as follows:

At the time the trustees bought the bonds they were worth about 60. Indeed, if the Union Pacific had thrown such a large amount of bonds onto a weak market, the market price would probably have fallen well below 60. The sale of bonds by the Union Pacific to the trustees at 60 was, therefore, not another device for draining the assets of the railroad out of the company and into the pockets of the promoters. It was not a cloak for increasing the sum total of the payments to the promoters for construction. Rather, it was an *equal value exchange* of one asset—bonds—for another asset badly needed by the Union Pacific—cash.

The gain realized on the transaction was entirely due to the fact that the securities appreciated in value *after* the trustees made the purchase. The gain on the transaction was thus a " security holder's " gain. During the period of construction, the promoters were involved in many such " security holder's "

[8] *Ibid.*, p. XVI.

gains and losses (as opposed to profit on construction). Such gains and losses took place when the promoters continued to hold the securities in which they were paid rather than immediately converting them into cash at the then prevailing market prices. For example, the promoters received a $3,000,000 stock payment on account of construction from the Union Pacific in July of 1870.[9] At the time Union Pacific stock was quoted at 28. A few months later the value of the stock fell to 10. Thus the promoters suffered a "security holder's" loss of about $600,000.

If the promoters had been paid in cash, issues of this sort would not arise. If they had been paid entirely in cash, the profit of the promoters would have been the difference between the cash payments made to them and their cash expenditures. What the promoters subsequently did with this cash profit, what later gains or losses they made in the handling of this money would have had no bearing on the estimate of the construction profit. It seems logical to follow a similar approach when part of the payment was in securities. The construction profit should be evaluated on the basis of the value of the securities *at the time the Union Pacific made the security payment.* The fact that the promoters did not immediately sell the securities at the prevailing market price and subsequently suffered losses or made gains due to a later depreciation or appreciation of the securities should not affect our estimate of the construction profit. The decision to hold rather than sell the securities was equivalent to a decision to enter a new enterprise—security holding. While the results of this decision certainly affected the financial standing of the promoters, it was an enterprise that was logically distinct from the enterprise of making profit by building the road.

If the rule of evaluating the profit of the promoters on the basis of the value of the securities at the time the Union Pacific made the payment is not followed, a host of imponderable questions arise. For example, when did the gain of $1,168,000 actually take place? Was it a real gain or just a paper gain? In real terms, did the promoters lose or gain from the exchange of assets with the Union Pacific? If we accept the Wilson committee estimate, the appreciation of the bonds took place

[9] Wilson, p. 750.

while the bonds were still held by the trustees. Thus, for the promoters as a group, the paper gain took place before the bonds were sold by the trustees; it took place while the bonds were held by the promoters' legal agent. The mere fact that the trustees sold the bonds to individual stockholders of the Credit Mobilier (i. e., that the promoters sold the bonds to themselves) did not convert the paper gain into a real gain. If it was only a paper gain when the trustees held the bonds for the promoters, it continued to be a paper gain when the bonds were transferred from collective to individual possession.[10] For the promoters as a group, the transaction became a real gain only when the individuals who possessed the bonds sold them to *outside* parties. If the individual promoters did not immediately sell the bonds to outsiders, the paper gain would have been converted into a paper loss as the value of the securities depreciated later in the year. Moreover, the promoters might have sold the bonds to outsiders during this period of depreciated prices. Then the paper loss would have been converted into a real loss. In this case, the net effect of having purchased the income bonds from the Union Pacific at 60 would not have been a real addition to profit but a real deduction from profit.

Practical as well as logical considerations are involved in the adoption of the rule suggested above. If the promotional profit is not evaluated on the basis of the prices of the securities that prevailed at the time the Union Pacific made its payments to the promoters, the promotional profit becomes indeterminate; one is confronted with as many profit figures as there were different security prices. Thus, if the prices of the securities that prevailed on June 6, 1870 are chosen as the basis for the evaluation, the upper limit on the profit of the promoters would be not 16.5 million dollars but 24.0 million dollars. If, on the other hand, the prices that prevailed on December 31, 1870 are chosen, the upper limit on the profit would be about five million dollars.

7). The same argument applies to the transaction on the land-grant bonds which led to a " holder's " gain of $165,000.

---

[10] However, the transfer from collective to individual possession did affect the distribution of the shares in the potential gain (or loss) among the various promoters.

8). While the 1869-1870 transactions did not affect the upper limit of the profit of the promoters, it did affect the lower limit. The trustees received a total of $5,222,000 in cash from the stockholders of the Credit Mobilier as a consequence of the bond sale. Of this amount, $3,889,000 replaced the cash that the trustees had used to buy the bonds from the Union Pacific. The differences between these two figures must be added to the cash fund out of which undisclosed expenses, if they existed, could have been paid.

APPENDIX B

DOCUMENTATION ON THE DISCOVERY AND ADOPTION OF THE EVANS PASS ROUTE

Oakes and Oliver Ames claimed that Evans pass, the easy route across the Rocky Mountains, did not become known to the promoters until after the signing of the Ames contract.[1] Most historians of the Union Pacific have either accepted this claim or reserved their opinion on it.[2] Henry Kirk White, for example, wrote: "Just when the character of the Evans Pass became known to the builders of the Union Pacific cannot be said. . . . It would be interesting to know whether or not knowledge of this easy route came before the letting of the next contract [the Ames contract] which we have to consider. . . . But unfortunately definite information as to this date is not forthcoming."[3]

Definite information on the date is contained in some neglected reports by the government directors of the Union Pacific to the Secretary of Interior. During the summer and early fall of 1866, a party of engineers, including government director J. L. Williams, surveyed possible routes over the Rocky Mountains. On November 23, 1866, Williams submitted a report which contained detailed descriptions of ten possible routes. One of these was the "Lodge Pole and Crow Creek line, over Evans's pass, designated as route No. 7."

In a report dated December 1, 1866, Williams wrote:

On the 23d November I had the honor to forward to you from New York a report of my late reconnoissance [sic.] over the preliminary lines run for the Union Pacific railroad across the first mountain range.

---

[1] Wilson, pp. 28, 252-54, and especially p. 255.

[2] An exception is John Deba Galloway, *The First Transcontinental Railroad* (New York: Simmons-Boardman, 1950), pp. 212-13.

[3] White, *op. cit.*, pp. 29-30. The Ames contract was adopted by the Union Pacific's executive committee on August 16, 1867. It was approved by the board of directors on October 1 of the same year. The trusteeship agreement was signed two weeks later. Wilson, part II, pp. 10-13.

At that date the important subject of definite location was before the committee on location and construction, by reference to them of the chief engineer's report, the question having been virtually narrowed down to the two available routes over the Black Hill range.

I now report that the committee, after mature deliberation, recommended the line designated in my descriptive report of the 23d ultimo, as "*Route No. 7*". . . .

A report dated January 7, 1867, and signed by all five government directors, contained the following important passage:[4]

The regular meeting of the board of directors of the Union Pacific Railroad Company was held last week, and the undersigned, government directors, submit for your information, on the condition and progress of the road, the following report:

Referring to the report of the government directors of September last, it was stated that our colleague, J. L. Williams, esq., was then making an examination with the chief and consulting engineers of this company, of the lines surveyed in the Rocky Mountain region, and his report on that subject has since been made and filed in your department.

The board of directors have adopted the location of the route via Lodge Pole creek, over the Rocky mountains at Evans's pass, to Laramie river, 580 miles from Omaha. (Emphasis mine.)

The promoters had more than a casual knowledge of the existence of Evans pass. They possessed detailed information on the technical advantages of the route. In his report of November 23, 1866, J. L. Williams wrote: The " length of expensive mountain line across the range, by the two [best] routes respectively, is by the Cache la Poudre 39¼ miles; by the Lodge Pole [Evans pass] 23¼ miles." In his report of December 1st, Williams wrote: " Its [Evans pass'] leading advantages over the Cache la Poudre route are, the saving of the distance, 37 miles, lower maximum grade by 15 or 20 feet per mile, lighter grading, facilitating the rapid extension of the track, and less obstruction from snow drifts, following as it does, on the eastern slope, a ridge instead of a valley."[5]

During the course of the Wilson hearings, Durant stated that the directors of the Union Pacific had had estimates of the cost

[4] All three reports are contained in *Sen. Exec. Docs.* No. 2, 40th Cong., Spec. Sess. (1308), pp. 20-24. The board meeting described in the January 7th report took place on January 5th. Oliver Ames attended the meeting. Wilson, p. 67.

[5] *Sen. Exec. Docs.* No. 2, *op. cit.*, pp. 21,24.

of building over the Rocky Mountains before the signing of
the Ames contract. " We had profiles from the engineers, and
estimates were made from the profiles by engineers and officers
here, so that we had an approximate estimate of a portion of
the work. There was no necessity of going into estimates of
the level portion." [6]

The following question was put to government director
Charles T. Sherman during the Wilson hearings: " Q. . . . Now,
I wish to ask you how fully the character of that route [the
Evans pass route], as described in the report which I have
shown you, was known to the direction of the Union Pacific
Railroad Company prior to the letting of the Oakes Ames
contract, on August 16, 1867?—A. My impression is that it
was fully known to the board of directors, and to the parties
interested in that contract." [7]

The final piece of evidence on the timing of the adoption of
Evans pass comes from the *American Railroad Journal* of
January 19, 1867, which reported that " the road [the Union
Pacific] is definitely located up the Lodge Pole creek to the
foot of the Black Hills, then through ' Evans' Pass ' to the
Laramie river, a further distance of near three hundred miles,
which it is contemplated to build during the present year." [8]

[6] Wilson, p. 89.
[7] *Ibid.*, p. 651.
[8] Vol. XL, p. 71.

SELECTED BIBLIOGRAPHY

Public Documents

Poe, Orlando Metcalfe, "History and Construction of Transcontinental Railways in the United States," U. S. House of Representatives, *Annual Report of the Secretary of War, 1883.* Executive Document No. 1. 48th Cong., 1st Sess. (2182).

U. S. Bureau of the Census. *Eighth Census of the United States: 1860. Statistics of the United States.*

——. *Eleventh Census of the United States: 1890. Report on Real Estate Mortgages,* Vol. XII.

——. *Eleventh Census of the United States: 1890. Report on the Statistics of Agriculture,* Vol. V.

——. *Tenth Census of the United States: 1880. Valuation, Taxation and Public Indebtedness,* Vol. VII.

U. S. *Congressional Globe.* Vols. XIV-XXXIV, 1845-1864.

U. S. House of Representatives. *Affairs of the Union Pacific Railroad Company.* Report No. 78. 42d Cong., 3d Sess. (1577).

——. *Annual Report of the Secretary of Interior, 1865-1868.* Executive Document No. 1. 39th Cong., 1st Sess.; 39th Cong., 2d Sess.; 40th Cong., 2d Sess.; 40th Cong., 3d Sess. (1248, 1284, 1326, 1366).

——. *Credit Mobilier Investigation.* Report No. 77. 42d Cong., 3d Sess. (1577).

——. *Letter from the Postmaster General Relative to Amount Paid the Union Pacific Railroad Company for Transportation of Mails in Each Year Since June 30, 1866.* Executive Document No. 151. 42d Cong., 3d Sess. (1567).

——. *Majority and Minority Reports of the Select Committee on the Pacific Railroad.* Report No. 428. 36th Cong., 1st Sess. (1069).

——. *Railroad to Oregon.* Report No. 733. 30th Cong., 1st Sess. (526).

——. *Whitney's Railroad to the Pacific.* Report No. 140. 31st Cong., 1st Sess. (583).

U. S. Senate. *Majority and Minority Reports and Testimony Taken by the United States Pacific Railway Commission.* Executive Document No. 51. 50th Cong., 1st Sess. 8 Vols. (2505-2509).

——. *Report of the Committee on Public Lands.* Report No. 466. 29th Cong., 1st Sess. (478).

——. *Report of the Committee on Roads and Canals.* Report No. 194. 31st Cong., 1st Sess. (565).

——. *Reports of the Government Directors of the Union Pacific Railroad Company.* Executive Document No. 2. 40th Cong., Spec. Sess. (1308).

——. *Reports of the Government Directors of the Union Pacific Railroad Company.* Executive Document No. 69. 49th Cong., 1st Sess. (2336).

Books

Asher and Adams' New Statistical and Topographical Atlas of the United States. New York: Asher and Adams, 1874.

Bailey, William Francis. *The Story of the First Transcontinental Railroad.* Fair Oaks, Cal.: W. F. Bailey, 1906.

Bancroft, Hubert Howe. *History of California.* Vol VII. Vol. XXIV of the *Works of Hubert Howe Bancroft.* San Francisco: The History Co., 1890.

Cleveland, Frederick A. and Powell, Fred Wilbur. *Railroad Promotion and Capitalization in the United States.* New York: Longmans, Green, and Co., 1909.

Cowles, Alfred, 3rd and Associates. *Common Stock Indexes.* Cowles Commission for Research in Economics. Monograph No. 3. 2d ed. Bloomington, Indiana: Principia Press, 1939.

Crawford, J. B. *The Credit Mobilier of America.* Boston: C. W. Calkins and Co., 1880.

Daggett, Stuart, *Chapters on the History of the Southern Pacific.* New York: Ronald Press, 1922.

————. *Railroad Reorganization.* Boston and New York: Houghton, Mifflin and Co., 1908.

Davis, John P. *The Union Pacific Railway.* Chicago: S. C. Griggs. and Co., 1894.

Dodge, Major General Grenville M. *How We Built the Union Pacific Railway and Other Railway Papers and Addresses.* N. p., n. n., n. d.

Donely, George Anthoney. *The Construction of the Union Pacific Railway by the Credit Mobilier of America.* Unpublished Master's essay, Columbia University, 1958.

Galloway, John Debo. *The First Transcontinental Railroad.* New York: Simmons-Boardman, 1950.

Goodrich, Carter. *Government Promotion of Canals and Railroads, 1800-1890.* New York: Columbia University Press, 1960.

Guide to Union Pacific Railroad Lands. Omaha: Land Dept., Union Pacific Railroad, 1872.

Haney, Lewis H. *A Congressional History of Railroads in the United States.* 2 Vols. Madison, Wis.: Democrat Printing Co., 1908, 1910.

Hazard, Rowland. *The Credit Mobilier of America.* Providence: Sidney S. Rider, 1881.

Kuznets, Simon. *National Product Since 1869.* New York: National Bureau of Economic Research, 1946.

Macaulay, Frenderick R. *The Movement of Interest Rates, Bond Yields and Stock Prices in the United States Since 1869.* New York: National Bureau of Economic Research, 1938.

Machlup, Fritz. *The Economics of Sellers Competition.* Baltimore: Johns Hopkins Press, 1952.

————. *The Political Economy of Monopoly.* Baltimore: Johns Hopkins Press, 1952.

Nevins, Allen. *The Emergence of Modern America, 1865-1878.* Vol. VIII of *A History of American Life.* Edited by Arthur M. Schlesinger and Dixon Ryan Fox. New York: Macmillan Co., 1932.

Paullin, Charles O. *Atlas of the Historical Geography of the United States.* Edited by John K. Wright. Washington, D. C. and New York: Carnegie Institution of Washington and American Geographical Society of New York, 1932.

Paxson, Frederic L. *History of the American Frontier, 1763-1893.* Boston and New York: Houghton Mifflin Co., 1924.

————. *The Last American Frontier.* New York: Macmillan Co., 1910.

Quiett, Glenn Chesney. *They Built the West: An Epoch of Rails and Cities.* New York and London: D. Appleton-Century Co., 1934.

Rand McNally's Pioneer Atlas of the American West. Historical text by Dale L. Morgan. Chicago, New York and San Francisco: Rand McNally and Co., 1956.

Riegel, Robert Edgar. *The Story of the Western Railroads.* New York: Macmillan Co., 1926.

Rhodes, James Ford. *History of the United States from the Compromise of 1850 to the Final Restoration of Home Rule at the South in 1877.* Vol. VII, 1872-1877. New York: Macmillan Co., 1920.

Russel, Robert R. *Improvement of Communication with the Pacific Coast as an Issue in American Politics, 1783-1864.* Cedar Rapids, Iowa: Torch Press, 1948.

Sabin, Edwin L. *Building the Pacific Railway.* Philadelphia and London: J. B. Lippincott Co., 1919.

Sheldon, Addison E. *Land System and Land Policies in Nebraska.* Vol. XXII of the *Publications of the Nebraska State Historical Society.* Lincoln, Nebraska: The Society, 1936.

Stigler, George J. *The Theory of Price.* New York: Macmillan Co., 1954.

Trottman, Nelson. *History of the Union Pacific.* New York: Ronald Press, 1923.

White, Henry Kirk. *History of the Union Pacific Railway.* Chicago: University of Chicago Press, 1895.

Articles and Periodicals

Adams, Charles F., Jr. "The Government and the Railroad Corporations," *North American Review,* CXII (January, 1871), pp. 36-61.

————. "Railroad Inflation," *North American Review,* CVIII (January, 1869), pp. 130-64.

————. "Railroad Problems in 1869," *North American Review,* CX (January, 1870), pp. 116-50.

American Railroad Journal. Vols. XVIII-XLVI. New York, 1845-1873.

Ashburner, S. "Railway Management," *North American Review,* CVI (January, 1868), pp. 43-67.

Colburn, R. T. "Pacific Railroad Grants," *Putnam's Monthly Magazine,* New Series II (October, 1868), pp. 488-95.

The Commercial and Financial Chronicle. Vols. I-XVII. New York, 1865-1873.

Davis, John P. "The Union Pacific Railway," *Annals of the American Academy of Political and Social Science,* VIII (September, 1896), pp. 46-91 (259-303).

Cotterill, R. S. "Memphis Railroad Convention, 1849," *Tennessee Historical Magazine,* IV (June, 1918).

————. " The National Railroad Convention in St. Louis, 1849," *Missouri Historical Review*, XII (July, 1918), pp. 203-15.

Goodrich, Carter. "American Development Policy: The Case of Internal Improvements," *Journal of Economic History*, XVI (December, 1956), pp. 449-60.

Hadley, Arthur T. " The Railroad in Its Business Relations," *Scribner's Magazine*, IV (October, 1888), pp. 473-88.

Ludlow, Fitz-Hugh. " Through-tickets to San Francisco: A Prophecy," *Atlantic Monthly*, XIV (November, 1864), pp. 604-17.

The Merchant's Magazine and Commercial Review. Vols. I-LXIII. New York, 1839-1870.

Paxson, Frederic L. " The Pacific Railroads and the Disappearance of the American Frontier," *Annual Report of the American Historical Association for the Year 1907*. Vol. I, pp. 107-18.

Poor, Henry V. " The Pacific Railroads," *North American Review*, CXXVIII (July, 1879), pp. 664-80.

" The Session," *North American Review*, CXVII (July, 1873), pp. 182-96.

INDEX

THE JOHNS HOPKINS UNIVERSITY
STUDIES IN
HISTORICAL AND POLITICAL SCIENCE

✶ ✶ ✶

SEVENTY-EIGHTH SERIES (1960)
(complete in two numbers)

I. The Nobility of Toulouse in the Eighteenth Century: A Social and Economic Study

By Robert Forster

II. The Union Pacific Railroad—A Case in Premature Enterprise

By Robert William Fogel

✶ ✶ ✶

THE JOHNS HOPKINS PRESS
BALTIMORE

THE JOHNS HOPKINS UNIVERSITY STUDIES IN HISTORICAL AND POLITICAL SCIENCE

A subscription for the regular annual series is $5.00. Single numbers may be purchased at special prices. A complete list of the series follows.

FIRST SERIES (1883)—Bound Volume.. O. P.

1. Introduction to American Institutional History, An. By E. A. Freeman..... .75
2. Germanic Origin of New England Towns. By H. B. Adams.......... O. P.
3. Local Government in Illinois. By Albert Shaw. Local Government in Pennsylvania. By E. R. L. Gould...... O. P.
4. Saxon Tithingmen in America. By H. B. Adams......................... .75
5. Local Government in Michigan and the Northwest. By E. W. Bemis.... .75
6. Parish Institutions of Maryland. By Edward Ingle..................... 1.00
7. Old Maryland Manors. By John Hemsley Johnson .... O. P.
8. Norman Constables in America. By H. B. Adams..................... .75
9-10. Village Communities of Cape Ann and Salem. By H. B. Adams....... 1.25
11. Genesis of a New England State. By A. Johnston .... O. P.
12. Local Government and Schools in South Carolina. By B. J. Ramage... 1.00

SECOND SERIES (1884)—Bound Volume O. P.

1-2. Method of Historical Study. By H. B. Adams...................... O. P.
3. Past and Present of Political Economy. By R. T. Ely.................... 1.00
4. Samuel Adams, the Man of the Town Meeting. By James K. Hosmer..... 1.00
5-6. Taxation in the United States. By Henry Carter Adams.............. 1.25
7. Institutional Beginnings in a Western State. By Jesse Macy.............. .75
8-9. Indian Money in New England, etc. By William B. Weedon............ 1.00
10. Town and Country Government in the Colonies. By E. Channing........ O. P.
11. Rudimentary Society Among Boys. By J. Hemsley Johnson................ O. P.
12. Land Laws of Mining Districts. By C. H. Shinn.................... O. P.

THIRD SERIES (1885)—Bound Volume. O. P.

1. Maryland's Influence Upon Land Cessions to the U. S. By H. B. Adams.. 1.50
2-3. Virginia Local Institutions. By E. Ingle .... O. P.
4. Recent American Socialism. By Richard T. Ely...................... O. P.
5-6-7. Maryland Local Institutions. By Lewis W. Wilhelm................ 2.00
8. Influence of the Proprietors in Founding New Jersey. By A. Scott....... .75
9-10. American Constitutions. By Horace Davis .... O. P.
11-12. City of Washington. By J. A. Porter .... O. P.

FOURTH SERIES (1886)—Bound Volume O. P.

1. Dutch Village Communities on the Hudson River. By I. Elting....... O. P.
2-3. Town Government in Rhode Island. By W. E. Foster. The Narragansett Planters. By Edward Channing...... O. P.
4. Pennsylvania Boroughs. By William P. Holcomb 1.00
5. Introduction to Constitutional History of the States. By J. F. Jameson.... O. P.
6. Puritan Colony at Annapolis, Maryland. By D. R. Randall............. O. P.
7-8-9. Land Question in the United States. By S. Sato .... O. P.
10. Town and City Government of New Haven. By C. H. Levermore....... 1.50
11-12. Land System of the New England Colonies. By M. Egleston.......... O. P.

FIFTH SERIES (1887)—$8.00

1-2. City Government of Philadelphia. By E. P. Allinson and B. Penrose....... O. P.
3. City Government of Boston. By James M. Bugbee...................... O. P.
4. City Government of St. Louis. By Marshall S. Snow................... .75
5-6. Local Government in Canada. By John George Bourinot............. 1.25

iii

v

vi

vii

2. Roman Rhetorical Schools as a Preparation for the Courts Under the Early Empire. By E. Patrick Parks....... 1.50
3. Slave States in the Presidential Election of 1860. By Ollinger Crenshaw. Paper 4.00; Cloth 4.50

〈XTY-FOURTH SERIES (1946)
1. Great National Project: A History of the Chesapeake and Ohio Canal. By W. S. Sanderlin...Paper 4.00; Cloth 4.50
2. Richard Hildreth. By Donald E. Emerson 2.75
3. William Rufus Day: Supreme Court Justice from Ohio. By Joseph E. McLean 2.75

〈XTY-FIFTH SERIES (1947)
1. British Block Grants and Central-Local Finance. By Reynold E. Carlson.... 3.25
2. Landowners and Agriculture in Austria, 1815-1848. By Jerome Blum....... 4.00

〈XTY-SIXTH SERIES (1948)
1. French Freemasonry Under the Third Republic. By Mildred J. Headings.. 4.50
2. Science and Rationalism in the Government of Louis XIV, 1661-1683. By James E. King................... 4.50

〈XTY-SEVENTH SERIES (1949)
1. Capitalism in Amsterdam in the 17th Century. By Violet Barbour....... O. P.
2. The Patent Grant. By Burke Inlow.. 2.50
3. Saint Mary Magdalene in Mediaeval Literature. By Helen Garth........ 2.00

〈XTY-EIGHTH SERIES (1950)
1. The Organization of State Administration in Delaware. By Paul Dolan... 2.50
2. The Theory of Inter-Sectoral Money Flows and Income Formation. By John Chipman......................... 2.50
3. Congressional Differences over Foreign Affairs, 1921-41. By George Grassmuck 2.75

Bound Volumes Discontinued Beginning with the Sixty-Ninth Series.

〈XTY-NINTH SERIES (1951)
1. Party and Constituency: Pressures on Congress. By Julius Turner........ O. P.
2. The Legates of Galatia From Augustus to Diocletian. By Robert K. Sherk.. 2.50

〈VENTIETH SERIES (1952)
1. Federal Examiners and the Conflict of Law and Administration. By Lloyd D. Musolf 3.00
2. The Growth of Major Steel Companies, 1900-1950. By Gertrude G. Schroeder ....Paper 4.00, Cloth 5.00

SEVENTY-FIRST SERIES (1953)
1. The Revolt of 1916 in Russian Central Asia. By Edward D. Sokol......... 3.25
2. Four Studies in French Romantic Historical Writing. By Friedrich Engel-Janosi 2.50

SEVENTY-SECOND SERIES (1954)
1. Price Discrimination in Selling Gas and Electricity. By Ralph Kirby Davidson ....Paper $3.00, Cloth 4.00
2. The Savings Bank of Baltimore, 1816-1866. By Peter L. Payne and Lance E. Davis ....Paper 3.00

SEVENTY-THIRD SERIES (1955)
The Paris Commune in French Politics, 1871-1880. By Jean T. Joughin. .... Two vols. ....Paper 7.50
1. Volume I: The Partial Amnesty
2. Volume II: The Final Amnesty

SEVENTY-FOURTH SERIES (1956)
1. Robert Oliver, Merchant of Baltimore, 1783-1819. By Stuart Weems Bruchey. Paper 5.00
2. Political Theory and Institutions of the Khawārij. By Elie Adib Salem. Paper 3.00

SEVENTY-FIFTH SERIES (1957)
1. Britons in American Labor: A History of the Influence of the United Kingdom Immigrants on American Labor, 1820-1914. By Clifton K. Yearley, Jr. 4.00
2. The Location of Yamatai: A Case Study in Japanese Historiography. By John Young ....O. P.

SEVENTY-SIXTH SERIES (1958)
1. Trends in Birth Rates in the United States since 1870. By Bernard Okun. 3.50
2. The Dynamics of Supply: Estimation of Farmers' Response to Price. By Marc Nerlove..........Paper 4.00; Cloth 5.00

SEVENTY-SEVENTH SERIES (1959)
1. Republicans Face the Southern Question—The New Departure Years 1877-1897. By Vincent P. De Santis. Paper 4.00; Cloth 5.00
2. Money, Class, and Party: An Economic Study of Civil War and Reconstruction. By Robert P. Sharkey. Paper 4.00; Cloth 5.50

SEVENTY-EIGHTH SERIES (1960)
1. The Nobility of Toulouse—An Economic Study of Aristocracy in the Eighteenth Century. By Robert Forster. Paper 3.50; Cloth 5.00
2. The Union Pacific Railroad—A Case in Premature Enterprise. By Robert William Fogel. .....Paper 3.00; Cloth 3.50